COUNTERING HATE

Leadership Cases for Nonviolent Action

KRISTINE F. HOOVER, ED.D.

Kendall Hunt
publishing company

Cover image © Shutterstock.com.

www.kendallhunt.com
Send all inquiries to:
4050 Westmark Drive
Dubuque, IA 52004-1840

Published in the United States of America

CONTENTS

FORWARD

Forward by Sally Kohn, activist and author of The Opposite Of Hate: A Field Guide To Repairing Our Humanity

What do we do about ideas we find despicable, even hateful—and, perhaps more to the point, what do we do about the people who espouse them? How do those of us who say we believe in equity and justice stand up against exclusion, intolerance and even violent forms of oppression without resorting to exclusion, intolerance and even violence ourselves?

In this simultaneously inspiring and practical book, Dr. Kristine Hoover challenges those of us committed to fighting hate to do so without accidentally replicating the values we say we oppose. Her call to principled, pacifist arms is eloquent and passionate. But she doesn't stop at lofty rhetoric. Because, as the saying goes, the road is made by walking it, Hoover paints compelling picture after picture of communities that stood together to fight specific instances of hate while doing so in ways that contribute to overall values and culture that undermines hate more systematically.

Hoover isn't judgmental about the other path. She's clearly sympathetic the justice-minded communities that have responded to violence and animosity with more violence and animosity. Hate doesn't just change the hater but the hated, dragging us all down. But Hoover shows us another way forward, with her compelling case studies of ordinary people who stood up to hate in extraordinary ways. She doesn't condemn those who took the other road, but she wants to make the high road seem ultimately more attractive in addition to making clear that it's more impactful as well. In this sense, Hoover is a lovely guide for those seeking a more loving world. She's not telling us what to do, she's simply sharing with us compelling stories of what others have done, what worked for them that might work for us.

Indeed, the through-line of this book couldn't be more relatable—the members of a community in northern Idaho coming together in response to neo-Nazis moving into their county, and together forming a nonviolent human rights organization that would go on to fight right extremism not only in Idaho but around the nation. Regular people, coming together to affirm their shared values in response to a crisis, ultimately helping inspire and instruct other regular folks to do the same thing. Which, in a sense, is what this collection does a public service through extending—retelling those stories and thus allowing them to spread even further, so that more and more people can stand up constructively and compassionately to mobilized hate.

Unfortunately, hate has always been deeply interwoven with our nation's past and present. And yet while arguably hate has become even more popular lately, urged on by reactionary voices doing everything they can to push back against even the slightest encroachments of equity, so too has it become popular to proclaim oneself against hate. We do so vocally and vociferously through society's new megaphone of social media, and through the older methods of t-shirts and lawn signs and bumper stickers, and even from time to time marching and chanting in the streets. But the real work of change—the real work of fighting not only this moment's manifestations of racism and misogyny and class discrimination and homophobia but also untangling the systems and institutions that perpetuate hate across generations—that is the quiet work of community organizing, working hand-in-hand together with our community to deconstruct hate and build in its place lasting policies, practices and cultures of equity and justice and compassion and interdependence and nonviolence. That is the patient, hard, lasting work outlined in the pages that follow—an invaluable road map for anyone hoping to blaze that path.

PREFACE

By Kristine F. Hoover, Ed.D.
Countering Hate: Leadership Cases for Nonviolent Action

Action supports future leaders in understanding time tested strategies to counter the rising levels of hate and division across the United States and work for greater justice. With the passing of Congressman John Lewis, we are reminded of how people from humble beginnings can inspire a nation. This text provides an academic resource for a new generation of leaders who want to work for freedom and equality with non-violent examples consistent with Congressman›s Lewis›s call to action: "When you see something that is not right, not fair, not just, you have to speak up. You have to say something; you have to do something."

President Abraham Lincoln signed the Emancipation proclamation on January 1, 1863, which declared "that all persons held as slaves" within the rebellious states "are, and henceforward shall be free." Dr. Martin Luther King, Jr. said that the 1964 Civil Rights Act was nothing less than a "second emancipation," referencing the Emancipation Proclamation. Today enlivening the work of freedom and justice for all and countering hatred requires and demands continued vigilance. The ten case studies presented in the text start with the rise of the hate group, the Aryan Nations, in Hayden, ID and include community responses to hate in Washington, Oregon, Montana, Wyoming, North Dakota, Tennessee, Pennsylvania, and North Carolina. The Aryan Nations originated in the secluded wilderness of Hayden, Idaho during the 1970s and attracted righteous Western-style anti-government patriots who were ready to take back what they perceived to be their God given White homeland and follow the teachings of Richard Butler and the Church of Jesus Christ Christian. Members of the Aryan Nations were attracted to scripture readings and the founding Fathers' documents, connected with the deeply held values of freedom from big government and self-sustainability and stressed their commitment and concern for the working-class man and his family. Aryan Nations followers began a spree of hate crimes and harassment that lasted for several decades, attacking people based on skin color, religious beliefs, and sexual orientation. Community members came together to form the Kootenai County Task Force on Human Relations and partnered with the Southern Poverty Law Center to bankrupt the Aryan Nations in 2000 by winning a $6.3 million civil judgment and have demonstrated sustained leadership in the work to stop hate over four decades.

Research on each of the cases presented recognizes that communities have a range of proactive and reactive strategies and the text delivers multiple examples of non-violent outcomes, persistence, and resiliency on the part of those who stand for the rights of justice, freedom and equality. In many ways, the book tells the story of local people who unified their towns and provided leadership that can inform actions of today and the future with state and federal legislative initiatives, celebratory activities, and counter-rallies at distant locations. Continuing the agenda of Dr. Martin Luther King, Jr., a fundamental lesson is that engaging with hate groups directly is counter to the nonviolent strategies proven in these case studies. Supporting free speech of all, while providing strength in numbers at counter-rallies with a broad range of leadership creates momentum toward community values and has time and again discouraged attitudes and norms that hatred in any manifestation is acceptable.

The book opens with an introduction that reminds readers of the violent outcomes and death of counter protestor Heather Heyer in Charlottesville, Virginia when community members and white supremacists clashed during the Unite the Right Rally in 2017. This sets the stage for the critical need to better understand non-violent actions that empowers communities without harm to persons or property. With this context in mind, readers will explore locations across the country and actions of community members to remain vigilant against hate motivated initiatives. Every case opens with a summary and timeline, provides points to ponder and discussion questions, and has links to the actual news stories and organizations relevant for the case. The closing chapter offers resources for communities to consider as they identify responses that are unique and contextualized for their specific needs. There is no one size fits all strategy, but rather a commitment to sharing options so that every town and city can build a culture of inclusion and act with solidarity.

A 2012 report titled "A Crucible Moment: College Learning and Democracy's Future," prepared by the National Task Force on Civic Learning and Democratic Engagement makes the case for colleges and universities to become more intentional about teaching civic engagement and preparing students to be active participants in democracy. This learning paradigm encourages connecting teaching and learning with outside the classroom, real-life experiences. The timing of the release coincides with the 20th anniversary of the fall of the Aryan Nations compound in Hayden, Idaho as well as the 40th anniversary of the creation of the Kootenai County Task Force on Human Relations.

"To carry out this work, we have determined never to remain silent. We can find no examples in history where silence has solved problems. Also, we will never engage in confrontation. We will follow the manner of Martin Luther King Jr. of doing something of our own elsewhere" - Tony Stewart, Founding member of the Kootenai County Task Force on Human Relations

This book is dedicated to my family for their patience, love, and support. It is also dedicated to each and every one of you, all ordinary people who have the choice to take action to counter hate and stand for the rights of freedom, justice, and equality and the power to continue the work of creating hate-free communities.

ACKNOWLEDGEMENTS

Thank you to everyone who has been a part of the journey to write these case studies, particularly my valued colleague Dr. Kem Gambrell, as we continue the work to educate future leaders that will stand against hate and build more inclusive communities. Students involved with the Gonzaga University graduate class Leadership Strategies to Counter Hate as well as graduate assistants and work studies researched the details, checked references, and helped to develop and pilot the discussion and quiz questions that bring these cases to life. I know that these leaders will continue their commitment to building more equitable and welcoming communities wherever their leadership may take them. I am grateful for your vision of a better, non-violent world.

Kell Anderson
Tiffany Collard
Sally Deck
Christy Dennler-Lusco
Jason Dunbar
Eileen Griffin
Avalyn Hine
Phatana Ith
Sharon Ohara
Caitlin Robertson
Michael Rorholm
Terri Jane Stewart
Julene Tegerstrand
Manojprabhakaran Thirupal
Veronica Veaux

ABOUT THE AUTHOR

Dr. Kristine F. Hoover is an Associate Professor at Gonzaga University in School of Leadership Studies, facilitating the Change Leadership concentration, and directing the Gonzaga Institute of Hate Studies. The Institute of Hate Studies bridges the academy with community engagement through research, teaching and partnerships with students, staff, faculty, and community members. She is a former Chair of the Washington Legislative Ethics Board and former Society for Human Resource Management (SHRM) trainer. Dr. Hoover earned a Master of Business Administration, Master of Organization Development, and Doctorate in Leadership Studies degrees from Bowling Green State University. Her research in applied ethics, diversity, and service learning has been published in a number of journals, including the *Journal of Business Ethics*, *Journal of Academic Ethics*, *Journal of Leadership Education*, *International Leadership Journal*, *Education + Training*, *Personnel Review*, and the *Organization Development Journal* and has been presented at the International Leadership Association (ILA), the Association of American Colleges and Universities (AAC&U), the Forum on Workplace Inclusion, the Midwest Academy of Management, and the International Network of Hate Studies (INHS).

Dr. Hoover is concerned with questions regarding how organizations and communities shape inclusion and cultures of dignity. "Why do we see some people through a lens of fear and others with an assumption of goodness or neutrality?" She became acutely aware of inequities when interviewing an African American nurse who shared stories about frequent experiences in the 1980s of people crossing to the other side of the street when they saw him coming. Even though she had walked the same paths, she had not been aware of anyone crossing the street just because they did not want to share the sidewalk with her. It was a formative experience that began opening her eyes to prejudice experienced as a part of some people's daily lives. While growing up with her grandparents on a dairy and grain farm, the dinner table had been shared with family and farm workers alike, regardless of background. Her parents are medical and education professionals, who modeled a commitment to caring and service. She was later also influenced by her mother-in-law, who started an immigrant education program in Ohio for people who came from Texas and Mexico to pick tomatoes. The children in these families did not have access to textbooks or consistent time to go to school, because they migrated with their families. These and many other formative experiences were framed by her family that taught her the importance of caring for one another, the value of diversity, and the inherent dignity in everyone.

The field of Hate Studies enquires into "the human capacity to define, and then dehumanize or demonize, an 'other,' and the processes that inform and give expression to, or can curtail, control, or combat, that capacity." The International Conference to Establish the Field of Hate Studies held in 2004, began a formal academic initiative to study hate, recognizing that there is limited research that brings together what is known from communication studies, criminal justice, education, history, law, leadership, management, philosophy, political science, psychology, religious studies, sociology and many other disciplines in an integrated or interdisciplinary effort to better understand and counter bias and bigotry in any of its manifestations. From the individual level of analysis to the systemic, from people who have been "other-ed" based on ability, age, ethnicity, gender identity, nationality, immigration status, religion, sex, sexual orientation, skin tone, or socio-economic status to a range of additional characteristics, and from emotions and attitude to genocide, Dr. Hoover invites you to be a part of the leadership needed for non-violent action to take action against hate.

Chapter 1

INTRODUCTION

The recent rise of hate in America is undeniable, but it is not a new phenomenon. What we are seeing is a resurgence of hate, of exclusionary and harmful beliefs and actions that view certain human beings as unworthy of human dignity and respect. By hate we mean "the human capacity to define, and then dehumanize or demonize, another" (The Gonzaga Institute of Hate Studies, n.d.). When we see others as less than ourselves (or ourselves as inherently better than others), if we lack empathy for other human beings, or do not treat people as we ourselves would want to be treated—that is dehumanizing or demonizing another. Hate includes all forms of bias and bigotry, including but not limited to ableism, ageism, anti-Semitism, classism, heterosexism, homelessness, Islamophobia, misogyny, religious animus, sexism, and xenophobia. Fundamentally, hate is antithetical to our pledge of allegiance "with liberty and justice for all."

The materials here provide case studies of how communities have empowered themselves to take nonviolent stands against hate and are not an exhaustive account of various hate incidents or hate groups. These nonfiction stories demonstrate how communities responded to White supremacy and White nationalism, beginning in the Pacific Northwest in the 1970s. They are relevant not only because of their geographic location, but also because of the lessons learned that have been utilized across the country to counter hate groups with nonviolent outcomes. While addressing root causes of inequity are critical, structural changes take time. And while societal level interventions are in process, individuals can also act now. These cases provide insights for abandoning helplessness and provide inspiration for those who would choose to stand for human rights.

These cases begin with work of the Kootenai County Task Force on Human Relations (KCTFHR), a community group who developed counter strategies in response to the Aryan Nations (About KCTFHR, n.d.). The Aryan Nations originated in the secluded wilderness of Hayden, Idaho during the 1970s and attracted righteous Western-style anti-government patriots who were ready to take back what they perceived to be their God given White homeland and follow the teachings of Richard Butler and the Church of Jesus Christ Christian (Aryan Nations/Church of Jesus Christ Christian, n.d.). Butler and his followers quoted scripture and the founding Fathers' documents, connecting with the deeply held values of freedom from big government and self-sustainability and stressing their commitment and concern for the working-class man and his family (Aryan Nations/Church of Jesus Christ Christian, n.d.).

These cases do not in any way represent a comprehensive set of examples of communities from across America who have consulted with the KCTFHR to counter hate with nonviolent strategies. We have selected these examples because they were identified as part of the "Northwest Territorial Imperative", one of the oldest and unsuccessful efforts to establish a Whites only homeland in Idaho, Oregon, Washington, Wyoming, and Montana or because the community (Pennsylvania, Tennessee, North Carolina, North Dakota) reached out for assistance from the KCTFHR.

Founding member of the KCTFHR Tony Stewart said that his dedication to the work of the Task Force comes in part from when he was a young boy growing up in the South. "I've always been so offended when people were treated in an unjust way" (Hult, 2011). One childhood incident in particular has stuck with him. While visiting relatives, his family heard an African American woman with a magnificent voice sing in church. His parents invited her to their church, but when they told the church elders of their invitation, the elders rejected it. The elders did not want an African American to share in their worship; Stewart considers this one of the foundational incidents that formed his perceptions about discrimination.

The resurgence of hate has been documented by hate crime reporting across the country, however underreporting remains a problem. The U.S. Justice Department's Bureau of Justice Statistics estimated there were an average of 250,000 hate crimes annually based on their National Crime Victimization Survey (Bureau of Justice Statistics, 2013), while the Federal Bureau of

Investigation (FBI) reported 7,120 criminal incidents in their 2018 Hate Crimes Report (Hate Crime Summary, 2019). While there are a number of reasons for these major inconsistencies, the underlying concern is the degree to which we as a society are committed to law and justice.

When our principles of governing, such as equality, inalienable rights, and free speech (Founding Principles and Virtues—Bill of Rights Institute, 2014) are challenged, there are too many examples of protests and counter-protests that have become violent. These may be clashes over the rights of people of color; rights of people who worship Judaism, Islam, or other religions; people who come from other countries; people who are gay; or people who have a disability. While hate crimes, defined by the FBI as harm to persons or property "motivated in whole or in part by an offender's bias against a race, religion, disability, sexual orientation, ethnicity, gender, or gender identity" (Hate Crimes, 2018) can be perpetrated by individuals, many times hate crimes are not lone wolf activities but are better understood as motivated by a "leaderless resistance" (Sweeney, 2017).

The concept of leaderless resistance is relevant to recognizing the significant role that hate groups play in hate crimes that may otherwise appear to be perpetrated by individuals. Although not the first to use the term, Louis Beam, a member of the Ku Klux Klan (KKK) and the Aryan Nations, published a manifesto in the 1980s that called for "leaderless resistance" to the U.S. government. He stated that only "very small or even one-man cells of resistance . . . could combat the most powerful government on earth" (Keller, 2018). Tom Metzger, a leader of the White Aryan Resistance, published "Laws for the Lone Wolf." Adding

> I am preparing for the coming War. I am ready when the line is crossed . . . I am the underground Insurgent fighter and independent. I am in your neighborhoods, schools, police departments, bars, coffee shops, malls, etc. I am, The Lone Wolf! (Burke, 2017).

There is reason for this decentralized strategy. Organized White supremacist groups like The Order and Order II committed high profile crimes during the 1970s and 1980s and the FBI began tracking the groups as militants (Jimison, 2018). The leadership resistance/lone wolf strategy skirts conspiracy statutes.

This is to say that hate groups do explicitly support the actions of what may seem like individuals who are inspired by their ideologies.

The work of the KCTFHR in countering hate has largely emerged from organized hate groups. White nationalist and White supremacy groups predicate their beliefs on the primacy of White Christian European descendants, generally dehumanizing or demonizing non-Christian, people of color, and or people who are gay. These groups have connections to earlier extremist movements, including the KKK, Aryan Nations, and Christian Identity (Anti-Defamation League, n.d.). Researchers and reporters have covered much about the Klan and many of its splinter groups, and while initial efforts to explore the Klan's history were grounded in the south, studies have expanded to include an understanding of White supremacy's context in the north, too. Regardless of geographic location, these hate groups are pursuing a range of strategies from race wars to normalization. Group such as Atomwaffen and Feuerkrieg Division clearly state their purpose is to prepare for a "race war" while others wear ties and run for political office (Anti-Defamation League, 2020).

When people are moved to act to *counter* hate, their actions can take many forms. These include *direct confrontation* by being in the physical presence of hate groups, bringing signs, chanting, and/or engaging in harm to persons or property (whether planned or unplanned). Violence between Klan and counter-protestors at an October 1997 rally in Asheville, North Carolina is an example of how direct confrontation also created extra publicity or what might be called free marketing for the hate group (Southern Poverty Law Center [SPLC], Avoiding Violence at Klan Rallies, 1998). About 30 members of the Klan marched through the streets of Asheville, North Carolina, wearing white robes and carrying Confederate flags. They were met by 1,000 counter-protestors who shoved and threw epithets and rocks at the Klan members. After the media coverage of the event, the Klansmen then scheduled another Asheville rally. These encounters can magnify publicity for hate groups and also raise concerns about the extremism of counter-protestors. The Westboro Baptist Church strategically antagonizes counter-protestors as a means to engage in law suits that have funded their enterprise. The very emotional nature of conflicting fundamental values can turn intentions of only being in the presence of those with whom there are essential disagreement to violent encounters, regardless of intentions not to engage. Based on the evidence provided in the cases presented here, violence by either protestors or counter-protestors is at best counterproductive, and at worst deadly.

Some community members would prefer a tactic of silence in response to hate groups because they are concerned that any counter initiative will damage the reputation of the community and have detrimental economic impacts. Other communities have identified a series of nonviolent strategies that allow people to act and to elevate their community's commitment to inclusion and diversity. The motto of The Byrd Foundation for Racial Healing is Stop the Hate, Educate. The Byrd Foundation provides training workshops, school visits, and community programs to combat the racism that lead to the 1998 horrific lynching of James Byrd Jr. The Byrd Foundation's efforts along with others, encouraged President Barack Obama to sign the Matthew Shepard and James Byrd Jr. Hate Crimes Prevention Act in 2009 (Deitle, 2019).

Before focusing on examples of nonviolent strategies in the cases in this text, we'll conclude this chapter by reviewing the violence that has too often occurred between protestors and counter-protestors when they comingle. Although there are many examples that could be considered, we will briefly examine the Unite the Right rally in Charlottesville, Virginia in 2017 (Heim, Silverman, Shapiro, & Brown, 2017), where a neo-Nazi killed one counter-protestor and injured 19 others. Two other examples of violent outcomes resulting from direct confrontation included here are the 2017 Charles Murry speech at Middlebury College and the 1981 bloodshed between the Invisible Empire and counter-protestors in Connecticut (Beinart, 2017).

2017: CHARLOTTESVILLE, VIRGINIA—COUNTERING THE UNITE THE RIGHT RALLY

Organizers of the 2017 Unite the Right Rally in Virginia stated that their goals included unifying the American White nationalist movement (Stapley, 2017), opposing the removal of the Robert E. Lee statue, and renaming the public park where the Robert E. Lee statue was located (Heim et al., 2017). While the Unite the Right rally was officially scheduled to begin at noon on Saturday, August 12, a group of White nationalists marched through the University of Virginia campus carrying lit tiki torches chanting Nazi-associated phrases including "blood and soil" (Keneally, 2018).

A broad range of counter-protestors were prepared to make a stand against White supremacy at the August 12 rally (Stockman, 2017). Some of the organizers of the counter-protestors were aware of the potential for physical danger and called for more people to participate in the counter-protests on site. A minister who was part of Solidarity Cville, sent a message with the following call prior to the rally: "There is an extremely high potential for physical violence and brutality directed at our community. We need your help—we don't have the numbers to stand up to this on our own" (Stockman, 2017). The group Congregate Charlottesville called for a thousand members of the clergy to counter-protest at the rally. The Charlottesville House of Prayer also came to the rally to pray (Suarez, 2017).

A broad range of counter-protesters engaged at the rally, including faith-based and civil rights groups, businesses and educational institutions. Many of the counter-protestors were individuals from Charlottesville who did not want to be silent in the face of hate, particularly since the Klan had just rallied in the city on July 8. Physical altercations occurred before noon August 12, and at 1:42 a 20-year-old Ohio man killed Heather Heyer and injured 19 others when he drove his vehicle into the crowd of counter-protesters. Heather Heyer was a 30-year-old woman who worked as a paralegal and lived in Charlottesville (Keneally, 2018). The perpetrator, a former teacher, was fascinated by Nazism and Hitler.

2017: MIDDLEBURY COLLEGE, VERMONT— COUNTERING A SPEECH BY CHARLES MURRY

Middlebury College in Middlebury, Vermont was founded in 1800 by the Congregationalists and is a small private liberal arts institution with just over 2,579 students. In the 2020 edition of the Best Colleges in National Liberal

Arts Colleges, Middlebury College is ranked number seven and the college is ranked number 10 of the Best Teaching Colleges in America (How Does Middlebury College Rank Among America's Best Colleges?, 2014).

Professor Allison Stanger, Ph.D., was a political scientist at the college. She was a liberal Democrat that strongly defended free speech on campuses and she held the role of one of the campus coordinators for speakers at Middlebury College, having moderated campus programs and speeches by liberal speakers without incident (Beinart, 2017).

On March 6, 2017, she hosted and moderated a speech by Libertarian political scientist and author Charles Murray on his 2012 book "Coming Apart" (Beinart, 2017). Murray earned his Ph.D. from the Massachusetts Institute of Technology (MIT) in political science. The SPLC identified Murry as a White nationalist and called his work "racist pseudoscience and misleading statistics [that] argue that social inequality is caused by the genetic inferiority of the black and Latino communities, women and the poor" (CenterSPLC, Charles Murray, n.d.).

The Murry speech was restricted to students, staff, and faculty with a maximum audience of 350 in the Wilson Hall. "We need to foster a climate where we can listen and respect differences," said Dean of Students Baishakhi Taylor. Taylor continued "We don't have to agree with everything. How do we engage in civil discourse?" "I would regret it terribly if my presence here today, which is an expression of support I try to give to all my students [. . .] is read to be something which it is not, an endorsement of Mr. Murray's teachings and writings," Middlebury College President Laurie L. Patton said to the students (DeSmet, 2017). Khan, a student and member of the American Enterprise Institute club that invited Murray to speak, was shouted down as he introduced Murray (DeSmet, 2017).

As Murry began his talk, several groups in the audience stood, turned their backs, and chanted "Who is the enemy? White supremacy," and "Charles Murray go away. Racist. Sexist. Anti-gay" (Miller, 2017). There were little to no efforts to stop the audience protests. "We believe that his views are racist. Our goal is not to give him a platform on this campus," student Emma Renai-Durning said (Syed, 2020).

Dr. Stanger was forced to relocate Murray to another room where she interviewed him via video that was streamed back into the McCullough Student Center where approximately 100 students and faculty remained in the audience. As Murray, Stanger, and then-Vice President of Communications Bill Burger left the building, their car was surrounded by a group of students. Violence broke out and Dr. Stanger received a serious concussion. She was forced to wear a neck brace and the seriousness of her injuries required months of recovery at a family home in Michigan to recuperate (Friedersdorf, 2017).

Forbes magazine named the 2017 visit as one of 10 moments that "capture a decade in education" (Finn & Kapp, 2020). Disciplinary actions were taken against 74 students and the incident sparked national debate about free speech on college campuses. The American Enterprise Institute (AEI) had invited Murray to campus and argued that preventing the talk was a violation of campus free speech policies. Murray's visit also encouraged a reevaluation of the college's protest policy.

In January 2020, the college announced that Murry would be returning to speak on campus in March of that year. The College Republicans extended the speaking invitation to discuss his book "Human Diversity: The Biology of Gender, Race, and Class" (Finn & Kapp, 2020). Open Campus Initiative was cosponsoring the event. 2020 would mark Murry's third trip to the campus, with his initial visit in 2007 when he talked about his 1994 book, *The Bell Curve*. Director of Media Relations Sarah Ray said that the college's speaker policy should not be interpreted as an endorsement or approval of the speaker's views and acknowledged the importance of open expression and student protest during speaker visits (Finn & Kapp, 2020). The Box Office Manager reported that the college has hired additional security for the event.

> Each year Middlebury hosts nearly 300 speakers who come to campus from across the country and around the world, invited either directly by the institution, by its faculty, or by its registered student organizations. With each event, we are committed to providing a forum in which the Middlebury community can engage in a thoughtful, rigorous, and respectful manner (Charles Murray Event, 2020).

1981: MERIDEN, CONNECTICUT—COUNTERING THE INVISIBLE EMPIRE

In 1980 and 1981, some in Connecticut considered the Invisible Empire to be inconsequential, with one person calling the group a "pathetic little band of bigots" (Hartford Courant, 1980). The Klan had come to the community for purposes of recruiting and to support police, who were being scrutinized over the shooting of an unarmed Black man. On March 21, 1981, approximately 1,000 people gathered to see the KKK march. Some of the counter-protestors carried rocks and bottles while police wearing full riot gear escorted the Invisible Empire marchers into City Hall (Connecticut History, 2019).

The Imperial Wizard, Wilkinson, wanted to return to the supporters in the crowd and it was determined that the Meriden police would escort the Invisible Empire in order for them to complete their march. The police flanked the Klansmen on both sides, but that did not stop angry people in the crowd from throwing bottles and bricks, among other items. Several of the marchers were bleeding from wounds inflicted by the flying objects. Police officers were also hit by the debris as they protected the Klan. Chants turned to "Kill the KKK in blue!" and "Cops and Klan work hand-in-hand" (Kosienski, 1981 as cited in Reed, 2017). Both the police and the marchers ran for protection in cars and drove away.

The violence did not stop after the police and marchers fled. Klan supporters and Klan protestors engaged in fist fights in the streets. Bystanders were hurt by flying objects. The brawling stopped within two hours of the initial flying objects and the crowds dispersed, leaving the streets littered with debris and shattered glass. Among the injured requiring medical treatment were 20 officers and four Klansmen. Someone had a concussion; another person lost a testicle and another person had to have a metal plate inserted into her head after being injured.

The story of the violence made the front page of newspapers including Sunday editions of the *Boston Globe, Los Angeles Times, Baltimore Sun,* and *New York Times.* The Klan's march agitated the counter-protestors and the attacks of the counter-protestors not only created a sense of sympathy and victimization for Klansmen but also framed the counter-protestors as violent extremistsOther outcomes of the violence included intimidating potential Klan supporters. Even Gary Piscottano, Grand Dragon in Scotland, left the Invisible Empire because it was too violent—"We don't want to start a race war," Piscottano told reporters (Defiance Crescent News Archives, 1981).

CONCLUSION

Unlike the tragic incidents of violence in Virginia, Middlebury College in Vermont, or the KKK Marches in Connecticut, the following cases are about communities that engaged nonviolent strategies to successfully counter hate. Much research is needed to better understand the root causes of and how to dismantle hate, addressing individual level issues of stereotypes and moral courage, in-group and out-group dynamics of exclusion and ostracism, and societal issues such as poverty and the wealth gap, acknowledging privileges that are experienced by some and not others. Healthy debate on the limits of free speech and hate speech need to be further explored. The right to march also merits further attention. There is much work to be done.

While all this work needs to be done, it can seem overwhelming to people who want to do something but are not sure what they can do. Stewart, founding member of the KCTFHR, has said that the work of responding nonviolently to hate will never be done.

> "The work is humbling," he reflected. "We've been empowered by the citizenry. We've been imaginative, and bold at times. We have much responsibility. We feel humble and grateful for the support we receive," he said. "There's incredible satisfaction to be involved with this" (as cited in Hult, 2011, p. 16).

Stewart continued, "Never forget why you exist," he said. "If you do, you will die. Be willing to take the criticism," he added. "You will be criticized, and you will be attacked" (Bowen, 2011).

Like many communities around the country, the communities in the cases presented here faced struggles between protestors and counter-protestors, free speech and hate speech, and who is included and who is excluded from belonging. These cases involve fliers and marchers, politicians, and media. The efforts to define the culture and values of any community, be they exclusionary or inclusionary, manifest through rallies and celebrations, holding political office, dropping literature, and putting up stickers. When people (or property) are harmed, the question becomes how to take a stand and not be silent in the face of these crimes.

In these cases, readers will find communities that acted when confronted with hate groups in their own backyards. At times struggling with fear, anger, and or frustration and rising to the occasions both reactively and proactively, the communities found multiple paths to unite and not be defined by bias and bigotry. These nonfiction accounts have taken place in states across the United States, from Washington to Pennsylvania. Anyone wanting to better understand a range of effective nonviolent community organizing actions to counter hate will find powerful inspiration here to stand for values of liberty and justice for all. Each case study will invite the exploration of how ordinary people can do extraordinary things to counter hate through vigilance and speaking out against threats to human dignity.

REFERENCES

About KCTFHR. (n.d.). Retrieved from www.idahohumanrights.org. https://www. idahohumanrights.org/about.html

Anti-Defamation League. (n.d.). *Christian identity.* https://www.adl.org/resources/ backgrounders/christian-identity

Anti-Defamation League. (2020, January 8). *White Supremacists embrace "Race War."* https://www.adl.org/blog/white-supremacists-embrace-race-war

Aryan Nations/Church of Jesus Christ Christian. (n.d.). Retrieved March 5, 2020, from Anti-Defamation League. https://www.adl.org/education/resources/profiles/ aryan-nations

Beinart, P. (2017, March 6). *A violent attack on free speech at Middlebury.* Retrieved from The Atlantic. https://www.theatlantic.com/politics/archive/2017/03/ middlebury-free-speech-violence/518667/

Bowen, H. (2011, November 7). *New human rights coalition taking shape.* Retrieved March 5, 2020, from Moscow-Pullman Daily News. https://dnews.com/local/ article_6db7fd9f-387d-57b8-a599-50319428593c.html

Bureau of Justice Statistics (BJS)—National Crime Victimization Survey (NCVS). (2013). Retrieved from Bjs.gov. https://www.bjs.gov/index.cfm?ty=dcdetail&iid=245

Burke, J. (2017, November 28). *The myth of the 'lone wolf' terrorist.* Retrieved from the Guardian. https://www.theguardian.com/news/2017/mar/30/myth-lone-wolf-terrorist

Charles Murray Event. (2020, January 22). *Middlebury college statement, Middlebury offices and services.* Retrieved March 8, 2020, from www.middlebury.edu.http://www. middlebury.edu/newsroom/campus-notes/node/642768

Connecticut History (2019, June 28). The Ku Klux Klan in Connecticut. https:// connecticuthistory.org/the-ku-klux-klan-in-connecticut/

Defiance Crescent News Archives, Jan 22, 1981, p. 17. (1981, January 22). Retrieved March 15, 2020, from NewspaperArchive.com. https://newspaperarchive.com/ defiance-crescent-news-jan-22-1981-p-17/

Deitle, M. C. (2019, March 6). The legacies of James Byrd Jr. and Mathew Shepard: Two decades later. *Police Chief.* Retrieved from Policechiefmagazine.org. https:// www.policechiefmagazine.org/legacies-byrd-and-shepard/

DeSmet, N. H. (2017, March 2). *Middlebury students disrupt* author. Retrieved March 5, 2020, from Burlington Free Press. https://www.burlingtonfreepress.com/story/news/2017/03/02/middlebury-students-shout-down-controversial-author/98629002/

Finn, J., & Kapp, C. (2020, January 22). *Charles Murray invited back to Middlebury by College Republicans.* Retrieved from The Middlebury Campus. https://middleburycampus.com/47898/news/charles-murray-invited-back-to-middlebury-by-college-republicans/

Founding Principles and Virtues—Bill of Rights Institute. (2014). Retrieved from Bill of Rights Institute. https://billofrightsinstitute.org/founding-documents/founding-principles/

Friedersdorf, C. (2017, March 6). *That's when the hatred turned on me.* Retrieved March 16, 2020, from The Atlantic. https://www.theatlantic.com/politics/archive/2017/03/middleburys-liberals-respond-to-an-protest-gone-wrong/518652/

The Gonzaga Institute for Hate Studies. (n.d.). Retrieved March 5, 2020, from www.gonzaga.edu. https://www.gonzaga.edu/academics/centers-institutes/institute-for-hate-studies

Hartford Courant. (1980, June 20). Connecticut's Klan?, 20., A1C, A8.Hate Crimes. (2018). Retrieved from Federal Bureau of Investigation.

Hate Crime Summary. (2019, November 12). Retrieved March 8, 2020, from FBI. https://ucr.fbi.gov/hate-crime/2018/resource-pages/hate-crime-summary

Heim, J., Silverman, E., Shapiro, R, T., & Brown, E. (2017, August 12). *Three dead in wake of clashes at Charlottesville white nationalist gathering.* Retrieved March 16, 2020, from https://www.inquirer.com. https://www.inquirer.com/philly/news/nation_world/Charlottesville-protest-white-nationalist-nazi-racism-violence-Trump.html

How Does Middlebury College Rank Among America's Best Colleges? (2014). Retrieved October 29, 2019, from @USNews. https://www.usnews.com/best-colleges/middlebury-college-3691

Hult, K. (2011, September). *Fig Tree—Kootenai County task force 30 years.* Retrieved from www.thefigtree.org. http://www.thefigtree.org/sept11/090711KootenaiTFHR.html

Jimison, R. (2018, August 21). *The death of a white supremacist leader.* Retrieved March 15, 2020, from CNN. https://www.cnn.com/2017/08/17/us/fbi-spying-white-supremacists-declassified/index.html

Keller, J. (2018, May 22). *There are no lone wolves.* Retrieved March 8, 2020, from Pacific Standard. https://psmag.com/news/there-are-no-lone-wolves

Keneally, M. (2018, August 8). *What to know about the violent Charlottesville protests and anniversary rallies.* Retrieved from ABC News. https://abcnews.go.com/US/happen-charlottesville-protest-anniversary-weekend/story?id=57107500

Miller, H. S. (2017, March 4). *If You're Pro-Gay but offend progressives, You're 'Anti-Gay'.* Retrieved from IGF Culture Watch. https://igfculturewatch.com/2017/03/04/youre-pro-gay-offend-progressives-youre-anti-gay/

Southern Law Poverty Center, Charles Murray. (n.d.). *Charles Murray.* Retrieved March 5, 2020, from Southern Poverty Law Center. https://www.splcenter.org/fighting-hate/extremist-files/individual/charles-murray

Southern Poverty Law Center, Avoiding Violence at Klan Rallies. (1998, March 15). *Avoiding violence at Klan Rallies.* Retrieved March 5, 2020, from Southern Poverty Law Center. https://www.splcenter.org/fighting-hate/intelligence-report/1998/avoiding-violence-klan-rallies

Stapley, G. (2017, August 14). *'This is a huge victory.' Oakdale white supremacist revels after deadly Virginia clash.* Retrieved March 15, 2020, from modbee. https://www.modbee.com/news/article167213427.html; https://www.splcenter.org/fighting-hate/extremist-files/individual/charles-murray

Stockman, F. (2017, August 14). Who Were the counterprotesters in Charlottesville? *The New York Times.* Retrieved from https://www.nytimes.com/2017/08/14/us/who-were-the-counterprotesters-in-charlottesville.html

Suarez, C. (2017, July 31). *Group calls for 1,000 faith leaders to protest Aug. 12 rally.* Retrieved March 15, 2020, from The Daily Progress. https://www.dailyprogress.com/news/local/group-calls-for-faith-leaders-to-protest-aug-rally/article_03c12494-7650-11e7-af2b-03239d27aa3a.html

Sweeney, M. M. (2017). Leaderless resistance and the truly leaderless: A case study test of the literature-based findings. *Studies in Conflict & Terrorism, 42*(7), 617–635. https://doi.org/10.1080/1057610x.2017.1407480

Syed, M. (2020, January 22). *Charles Murray, whose 2017 visit sparked violent protest, invited back to Middlebury College.* Retrieved March 5, 2020, from Burlington Free Press. https://www.burlingtonfreepress.com/story/news/local/2020/01/22/charles-murray-invited-back-middlebury-college-last-visit-students-protest/4545329002/

Chapter 2

THE STORY IN IDAHO
(1980s AND 1990s)

OVERVIEW

In 1973, Richard Butler purchased land and later set up a compound in northern Idaho that would become home to his neo-Nazi groups, the Aryan Nations, and Church of Jesus Christ Christian (Southern Law Poverty Center, Richard Butler). Their intimidation, harassment, and threatening tactics escalated to hate crimes beginning in December 1980 and continued for several decades (Walkin, 2004). In response, local community members created the Kootenai County Task Force on Human Relations (KCTFHR) in 1981, adopting a nonconfrontational approach that focused on victim support, organizing counter events during hate group activities, promoting state and federal human rights legislation, and coordinating educational programs and community events to advance human rights (About KCTFHR, n.d.). According to still active founder Tony Stewart, "To carry out this work, we have determined never to remain silent. We can find no examples in history where silence has solved problems. Also, we will never engage in confrontation. We will follow the manner of Martin Luther King Jr. of doing something of our own elsewhere" (Hult, 2011, p. 1).

Timeline

1981	Founding of the Kootenai County Task Force on Human Relations (Coeur d'Alene, Countering hate graffiti and harassment)
1986, July	Five-State Rally (Coeur d'Alene, Countering Aryan Nations World Congress)
1986, September	"Gathering for Solidarity" (Coeur d'Alene, Countering hate bombings)
1989, April	20th Birthday Party for Idaho Human Rights Commission (Coeur d'Alene, Countering skinhead conference)
1990s	Initially a Time for Awards, Celebrations, Collaborations, Camps, and More Anti-Hate Work . . . (Coeur d'Alene, Countering hate graffiti and literature)
1998, January to July	"Lemons to Lemonade," "In It Together," and "Hands Across the Border for Human Rights" (Coeur d'Alene, Countering a hate march)
1999, July	Rally to Celebrate Human Rights for All People (Coeur d'Alene, Countering a hate march)

1981: FOUNDING OF THE KOOTENAI COUNTY TASK FORCE ON HUMAN RELATIONS

In 1973, Richard Butler, a former aeronautical engineer, and his wife Betty purchased 40 acres of land and set up a compound in northern Idaho for his neo-Nazi groups, the Aryan Nations, and Church of Jesus Christ Christian. Their intimidation, harassment, and threatening tactics escalated to hate crimes beginning in December 1980 (Southern Law Poverty Center, Richard Butler). In December, Butler's associates targeted a Jewish-run restaurant in Hayden, Idaho, defacing it with swastikas. In February 1981 and March 1983, a member of the Aryan Nations harassed and threatened a bi-racial family with four children in Coeur d'Alene. The city attorney prosecuted the Aryan Nations' member for a misdemeanor under Idaho's verbal assault law and on October 24, 1983 the party was found guilty and sentenced to served 60 days in jail (Hult, 2016). (Wassmuth and Gissel were not at the first meeting.)

The Jewish restaurant incident and others motivated local citizens to create the KCTFHR in February 1981, fewer than 10 members including activist Diana Tanners (who came to be known as the mother of the Task Force), Kootenai County Undersheriff Larry Broadbent, realtor Marshall Mend, North Idaho College Political Science faculty member Tony Stewart, met that night at the First Christian Church in Coeur d'Alene. The priest of St. Pius X Catholic Church, Fr. Bill Wassmuth, and Attorney Norm Gissel joined in 1984 (Hult, 2016). The group operated on three democratic principles: freedom, equality, and justice, focusing on supporting victims of hate crimes or harassment and opposing discrimination. The small group that met that February night at the First Christian Church in Coeur d'Alene, Idaho to determine how to counter the hate crimes that had cropped up in and around Kootenai County and Rick Morse, pastor of First Christian Church, took on the role of president. Six members of the Aryan Nations also attended, marching silently in the back of the room during the meeting (Hult, 2016).

These citizens and the newly formed KCTFHR told Sid Rosen, the owner of the defaced restaurant, they would take action when there was organized bigotry in their community. Mend said "We felt we needed a new law." For Mend, reflecting on his motivations, he said:

> "I had never been involved in human rights. I liked all kinds of people. I had a variety of friends. In the early 1960s, my first wife used to march in civil rights protests, but I was working and did not get involved. At first, I was concerned about my family and myself, but that's when I changed. I was angry that someone would do that to four children and a single mother. That's when I made my commitment to human rights" (Hult, 2016, p. 8).

HEADLINE

Acts of hate and harassment helped spark commitment to promote human rights

Rick Morse and his family were harassed and threatened for his involvement as the KCTFHR president and the Task Force began to meet less frequently after the KCTFHR was successful in March 1983 with the passage of the Idaho Malicious Harassment Law. Then a syndicated cartoon picturing Adolph Hitler leaning against a sign that said "Welcome to Hayden Lake, Idaho" appeared nationwide (Hult, 2016). Mend saw the cartoon in the Long Beach Press Telegram in California. He and Sandy Emerson, head of the Coeur d'Alene Chamber of Commerce, reconvened the Task Force, asking Fr. Bill Wassmuth to lead the group in the spring of 1984. Fr. Wassmuth had no spouse or children and lived in a brick house, which they believed would keep him safe from bombing (Hult, 2016).

In late 1983, Larry Broadbent, Kootenai County Undersheriff and a KCTFHR founding member, discovered the presence of The Order near Metaline, Washington and informed Federal Bureau of Investigation (FBI) Special Agent Wayne Manis (KCTFHR History, n.d.). The Order (also known as Brüder Schweigen [German for Brothers Keep Silent], the Silent Brotherhood or the Aryan Resistance Movement) was created based on William Luther Pierce's novel The Turner Diaries (McCary, 2006). Founded by Robert Jay

Mathews, goals of the Order were to establish a Whites only homeland known as the Northwest Territorial Imperative. The Order's funding came from theft, counterfeiting, and robberies and on July 19, 1984, near Ukiah, California, they robbed a Brink's armored car for $3.6 million (U.S. Department of Justice, 1985). On June 18, 1984, radio talk show host Alan Berg was murdered in front of his home in Denver by Bruce Pierce and other Order members (Smith, 2017). Law enforcement traced Mathews to Whidbey Island in December of 1984 where he refused to surrender and died when the location where he was hiding burned down. Multiple members of the Order were jailed, with sentences as long as 252 years (Pankaatz, 2010).

In this context, Tony Stewart, founding member of the KCTFHR, became producer of the North Idaho College PBS TV Public Forum (1972–2008). The television shows and documentaries aired across the Pacific Northwest and Canada and today remain housed in the North Idaho College Molstead Library on the Coeur d'Alene campus (McAlister, n.d.). During September 23 to 27, 1985, North Idaho College and the KCTFHR cosponsored the symposium "Racism: Prejudice and Progress." More than 4,500 people attended the weeklong event with major civil rights leaders from diverse communities across America (KCTFHR History, n.d.).

© Atomazul/Shutterstock.com

Several anti-hate initiatives came to be in 1986. January saw the first of what would become an annual "Dr. Martin Luther King, Jr. Children's Week" for all fifth-grade students in Post Falls and Coeur d'Alene, Idaho. The efforts were spearheaded by Doug Cresswell, superintendent of the Coeur d'Alene School District and KCTFHR member, and Pam Pratt, Coeur d'Alene School District administrator and KCTFHR member (KCTFHR History, n.d.). There were visits from well-known civil rights speakers throughout the week as well as a culminating formal program. A five-statecollation was founded based on the KCTFHR bringing together groups from the five Northwest states of Wyoming, Oregon, Washington, Idaho, and Montana, named the Northwest Coalition Against Malicious Harassment (NWCAMH), which existed from 1986 to 2003. And since 1986, the KCTFHR has staffed a booth at the North Idaho Fair and Redo during the last week of August, where they present human rights materials and activities to some of more than 70,000 fair goers each year (KCTFHR History, n.d.). All of these efforts were to create greater visibility and support for a culture of inclusivity.

> **POINTS TO PONDER**
>
> Reflect on the strategies the community enacted to address the hate promoted by the Aryan Nations. Do you think that these were effective strategies? What would you have done if you were in this situation?

1986: FIVE-STATE RALLY

The KCTFHR learned that the Aryan Nations World Congress would be held on July 12 and 13, 1986 at the compound outside of Hayden, Idaho (KCTFHR History, n.d.). As a response and counter narrative to define values, Norm Gissel, the KCTFHR attorney and member, drafted a resolution in support of the Declaration of Independence, the U.S. Constitution, the state's constitution, and the rights and equality of all citizens in the Inland Northwest (Stewart & Gissel, n.d.). The resolution was sent to every mayor, city council, and county commission in five states (Idaho, Washington, Oregon, Wyoming, and Montana), asking each to pass their own resolution or proclamation.

Gissel's resolution was accompanied by a cover letter signed by Gissel, Coeur d'Alene Mayor Raymond Stone, and Kootenai County Commission Chair Frank Henderson. Two hundred cities and counties representing four million people adopted the resolution or issued a similar proclamation (Wassmuth & Bryant, 2002). Butler's World Congress on July 12 and 13 involved speeches, Nazi-style salutes, and a cross-burning with men in uniforms (some with masks and swastika armbands) patrolling the grounds holding automatic rifles. The audience included working-class men, women, and children. Some attending the event were concerned with the show of force and its impact on recruiting future members, saying "We have to reach beyond the run-of-the-mill jerk who's happy just to vote conservative every four years. But dressing up in sheets and yelling 'Heil Hitler' is just stupid, it just turns people off." Recognizing the appeal to American values by the Aryan Nations, another person attending the event expressed concern that the prominence of guns and Nazi and Klan regalia were "un-American, stating 'It Turns People Off' (Paterson, 1986).

Butler told a reporter "We're basically working toward a return to the kind of country our forefathers wanted when they came over on the Mayflower. You know yourself that today a white male is considered a third-class citizen by the de facto government, therefore, as the posterity of those who founded this country, it is our duty to reclaim our heritage." He went on to say "Ever since the silver mines collapsed the entire economy has been based on white in-migration. They come out which all kinds of evasive, weasely reasons why they came, but when you pin them down it's because they want to live with white people and educate their children with white people" (Paterson, 1986).

The Hayden Lake Fire Department regulations did not address cross burning and the department issued the bonfire permit for the Aryan Nations gathering. Police officers were stationed on the roads to photograph license plates and passengers on July 12, however, Larry Broadbent, Undersheriff for Kootenai County and member of the KCTFHR, said that the Aryan Nations meeting did not cross any legal boundaries (Paterson, 1986).

At the same time on July 12, 1986, the KCTFHR organized a "Coeur d'Alene City Park Human Rights Rally" with over 1,000 people in attendance from the five Northwest states as a counter event to the Aryan Nations World Congress (KCTFHR History, n.d.). The keynote address at the human rights rally was given by Idaho Governor John Evans, with proclamations of support from the other four Northwest governors. During Bill Wassmuth's speech, he coined the slogan "Saying 'YES' to Human Rights is Saying 'NO' to Racism." He later changed the slogan to "Saying 'YES' to Human Rights is the Best Way to Say 'NO' to Prejudice and Bigotry" (Powers, 2001, p. 26). Today the slogan still appears on KCTFHR literature. The event was rounded out with musical performances, dance, food, and sand painting on the beach of Lake Coeur d'Alene. The governor's message praised the community's commitment to diversity and condemned the efforts to create a separate Aryan homeland in Washington, Oregon, Idaho, Montana, and Wyoming. The adopted resolutions and proclamations initiated by Gissel and penned by the two hundred cities and counties representing four million people were on display at the rally (Wassmuth & Bryant, 2002). Also central to the success were the 40 media outlets from around the United States as well as the "Guardian" from England, which covered the events. Each journalist received a media package from the KCTFHR telling the story of human rights work and activities in the Inland Northwest as a counter to the Aryan Nations messaging (KCTFHR History, n.d.).

1986: "GATHERING FOR SOLIDARITY"

Angered by the success of the July 12th human rights rally, a hate group known as Order II bombed the home of the president of the KCTFHR, Fr. Bill Wassmuth. Late at night on September 15, 1986, Fr. Wassmuth was sitting in his living room talking with a friend in Seattle when a pipe bomb went off in a garbage can at the back of Wassmuth's house. The bomb ripped out the kitchen wall, perforated the ceiling and pieces of the house landed on a neighbor's house across the street; fortunately, Fr. Wassmuth was not injured (Woo, 2002).

Although the community was outraged, Fr. Wassmuth and the KCTFHR urged the citizens to refrain from violence. The KCTFHR organized a community rally in support of Fr. Wassmuth titled "Gathering for Solidarity" on September 25 at North Idaho College with Idaho Governor John Evans as the keynote speaker. Norm Gissel, the attorney for KCTFHR, penned a letter to the public that appeared in the *Spokesman-Review* newspaper on behalf of the human rights group the day before the unity rally and encouraged what became an overflow crowd in support of Fr. Wassmuth at the rally. The letter read:

The bombing of Father Bill Wassmuth's home Sept. 15 was a brutal and vicious attempt by racial terrorists to take Bill's life.

But it was more than that, more even than an assault on the KCTFHR to quell its voice and blunt its spirit. This bombing was an attack on our city, our county, our community and our way of life.

The racial terrorists who planned the bombing, made the bomb, drove to Father Bill's home, set the bomb next to his home, detonated the bomb, and stole away in the night, had more motive than the death of one parish priest. The terrorists want all of us to feel fear of that explosion, to carry with us that fear in our daily lives, and because of that fear, to cease our commitment as a community to equality of all races and tolerance of all religions.

Our community is placed at a crossroad by the bombing. How we respond as a community will be watched closely by the terrorists and by the rest of our country.

Will we bow silently to the terrorists' bomb or will we stand fast, confident in our beliefs and our way of life?

We have an opportunity to demonstrate our community resolve to the crisis thrust into our lives by this bombing, an opportunity not to express our outrage, anger and hostility toward any one group or any one terrorist or act of violence, but instead an opportunity to channel those feelings into a deeper understanding of the dignity of all people and to come closer together as a community now victimized by its first terrorist attack.

The Task Force is holding a "Gathering For Solidarity" at the Bonner room of the North Idaho College Student Union from 7 to 8 p.m. on Thursday, September 25. We should all be there.

(T. Stewart, personal communication, August 19, 2019).

On the morning of September 29, bombs were set off in downtown Coeur d'Alene at a luggage store and the Federal Building. Two other bombs failed to ignite. The perpetrators, Robert Pires, Olive, and Ed Hawley and Aryan Nations Security Chief David Dorr, were arrested and charged by law enforcement (Associated Press, 1986).

With the swell of action to protect human rights during 1986, 1987 saw the City of Coeur d'Alene receive the Raoul Wallenberg Civic Award (New York City). The award was accompanied by a generous financial gift that was used to establish a human rights collection including a children's section at the City of Coeur d'Alene Library. Also during 1987, 3,200 feet of the NIC Coeur d'Alene Lake Beach was dedicated to the Coeur d'Alene Tribe at ceremonies organized by the North Idaho College Board of Trustees, the KCTFHR, and Idaho Governor Cecil Andrus. The Coeur d'Alene Tribal Council chose the name "Yap-Keehn-Um Beach" (The Gathering Place); the beach is open to the public for their enjoyment (KCTFHR History, n.d.).

1989: 20TH BIRTHDAY PARTY FOR IDAHO HUMAN RIGHTS COMMISSION

Richard Butler had planned to host his first racist skinhead conference for youth on April 20, in which they would celebrate Adolph Hitler's birthday and Hitler's life. The KCTFHR decided to organize counter activities with a full week of events titled "The Human Rights Week of Celebration" during April 17 to 23, 1989 (KCTFHR History, n.d.).

On Monday, April 17, the KCTFHR invited supporters to visit the Task Force booth on the campus of North Idaho College to pick up orange ribbons. The request was to display the ribbons throughout the week on the side mirrors of cars, at businesses, on clothing lapels, and to be placed on trees around Coeur d'Alene. Over 6,000 ribbons were distributed during the early part of the week (T. Stewart, personal communication, August 19, 2019).

On Monday afternoon, North Idaho College and the KCTFHR hosted a party to celebrate the 20th birthday of the Idaho Human Rights Commission. The party included 600 fifth-grade students present from the Coeur d'Alene School District. Students waved balloons in the Boswell Hall Performing Arts Center, with Idaho Governor Cecil Andrus and State Senator Phil Batt, the authors of the 1969 bill that created the Idaho Human Rights Commission, and Executive Director of the Idaho Human Rights Commission Marilyn Shuler, who all gave celebratory speeches honoring the Commission's birthday. KCTFHR volunteers served pieces of a 20-foot long cake to the students at the end of the celebration (KCTFHR History, n.d.).

On the following Saturday, the KCTFHR hosted what was known as a country western cowgirl/cowboy human rights picnic in Rathdrum, Idaho. The week concluded with a Sunday afternoon interfaith service at St. Pius X Catholic Church in Coeur d'Alene with messages of hope, dance, music, and readings (KCTFHR History, n.d.).

1990s: INITIALLY A TIME FOR AWARDS, CELEBRATIONS, COLLABORATIONS, CAMPS, AND MORE ANTI-HATE WORK . . .

In 1990, the city of Coeur d'Alene became the first city in the state of Idaho to be honored with the highly distinguished "All American City Award." It was also in 1990 that KCTFHR began hosting an annual January gala to celebrate the national Dr. Martin Luther King, Jr. holiday. Becoming an active member of the Greater Coeur d'Alene Area Chamber of Commerce was a new strategy for the KCTFHR starting in 1990 (KCTFHR History, n.d.).

During 1991, the KCTFHR played a role in establishing the North Idaho College Human Equality Club, which lasted through 2008 and had one of the largest student club memberships on campus. It was also in 1991 that along with the Spokane Inter-Faith Community, the KCTFHR cosponsored a P.E.A.C.E. (People Everywhere Are Created Equal) Camp for Spokane and Kootenai Counties' high school students. The camp was free to the students and directed by Peggy Federici, Ph.D., professor of sociology and education at North Idaho College. The camp operated for 15 years (KCTFHR History, n.d.).

In May of 1991, after several incidents of the distribution of hate literature and the surfacing of anti-Semitic graffiti that read "Stop the Jew world order" on a concrete highway barrier near Hope, Idaho, local citizens of the city of Sandpoint and Bonner County invited Bill Wassmuth, executive director of the Seattle based NWCAMH and former president of the KCTFHR, to speak to the issue at a rally in Sandpoint, Idaho. Wassmuth, accompanied by members of the KCTFHR, spoke to over 300 residents at the local high school gymnasium urging them to be aware of the doctrine and actions of White supremacists in the area (Hammond, 2015). Aryan Nations leader Richard Butler along with a handful of his members attended the event. Marshall Mend, a cofounder of the KCTFHR, also addressed the audience and urged action. The urgency for the establishing of a local human rights organization in Sandpoint and Bonner County became clear on August 21, 1992, during the 11-day standoff with Federal law enforcement at the Ruby Ridge mountain cabin of Randy Weaver, a White separatist, on a warrant for his arrest on a gun charge. The standoff ended with the tragic death of Weaver's wife and son and a U.S. marshal.

On December 9, 1992, a group of citizens announced the official formation of the Bonner County Human Rights Task Force (BCHRTF) with the Rev. Mary Robinson as the first president. By the mid-1990s, the newly formed BCHRTF faced a major challenge when R. Vincent Bertollini and Carl Story, two wealthy California businessmen, moved to Sandpoint and established the 11th Hour Remnant Messenger, a Christian Identity White supremacy church. They began a campaign of massive mailings of hate literature. One mailing included anti-Semitic booklets and 6-foot-tall colored posters (Lalley, 1999).

> Racist Plans Move To North Idaho Ex-KKK Leader Is Considered One Of Nation's Most Active And Most Dangerous Militants

In October 1993, the KCTFHR, the American Council of Learned Societies, the International Research and Exchanges Board, and North Idaho College cosponsored the fourth in a ten-year series of conferences on the future of international human rights. The October 29–31, 1993 conference topic was

"Empowering Women: Achieving Human Rights in the 21st Century." The conference drew 900 delegates from around the world. The first conference had been held at The University of California at Berkley; the second conference was held in Moscow, Soviet Union; and the third conference was held at Columbia University in New York City (KCTFHR History, n.d.)

However, there was evidence of people still responding to Butler's invitations to make the Northwest home for White supremacists, separatists and Christian Identity followers. In 1995, Louis Beam purchased land east of Sandpoint, Idaho. Bo Gritz, developed land he called "Almost Heaven" near Kamiah, Idaho, and David Barley, moved his pro-White Christian Identity church from Arizona to Sandpoint (Keating, 1995).

On April 1, 1996, two bombs were detonated, one at The *Spokesman-Review*'s Valley office and a local U.S. Bank branch. A letter with White supremacy statements was left at the bank robbery and included the signature of the Phineas Priesthood. Members of the priesthood defined themselves as duty bound to murder people for "disobeying God's laws" on abortion, homosexuality, race-mixing and other "crimes." In 1994, Paul Hill, a Presbyterian minister, murdered an abortion-clinic doctor and escort in Florida and used Bible passages about the priest named Phineas to justify the killings. Phineas killed two sinners with a single spear and became a symbol of righteousness. The Phineas Priesthood used the story as justification against race-mixing. Three months later on July 12, armed masked men in fatigues bombed a Planned Parenthood clinic. The bomb buckled sheetrock, blew out ceiling tiles, and destroyed the concrete floor inside the entrance. The bombing happened moments before the same U.S. Bank branch bank that was bombed and robbed in April was robbed again (Morlin & White, 1996)

In August 1996, Norm Gissel, attorney and board member of KCTFHR, received a call from one of his clients. Over lunch the client identified the Phineas Priesthood members responsible for both the bombings of the *Spokesman-Review* and Planned Parenthood buildings in Spokane Valley and robberies. Gissel and his client took the information to the FBI and the bombers/bank robbers were arrested and convicted (KCTFHR History, n.d.)

In 1997 to 1998, as a proactive strategy to promote human rights, the North Idaho College Board of Trustees signed a nine-point agreement with the

Coeur d'Alene Tribe to promote and advance educational opportunities at the College. The KCTFHR was present for the signing and praised the College and the Coeur d'Alene Tribe for this significant agreement (Coeur d'Alene Tribe and North Idaho College 9 Point Agreement, 2018)

1998: "LEMONS TO LEMONADE," "IN IT TOGETHER," AND "HANDS ACROSS THE BORDER FOR HUMAN RIGHTS"

In January 1998, the KCTFHR learned that not only would the Aryan Nations hold their annual Aryan Nations World Congress in July at the compound on the Rimrock above Hayden, Idaho, but for the first time they would apply for a parade permit to march on Sherman Avenue, the main street in Coeur d'Alene, on Saturday, July 18 along with fellow White supremacists including the Ku Klux Klan (KKK) (Struck, 2017). The KCTFHR decided to organize a series of counter events and activities in partnership with community activists, organizations, and institutions (KCTFHR History, n.d.).

Tony Stewart, KCTFHR founding member, was already scheduled to give a speech at the Magnuson Club. At the luncheon and later at a KCTFHR press conference, Stewart outlined the Task Force's Lemons to Lemonade project, inviting people to pledge money per minute that the Aryan Nations marched (Anti-Hate Drive Exceeds $35,000, 1998). The Task Force would turn a sour situation (the Aryan Nation's march) into something good (fundraising for human rights education), ergo Lemons to Lemonade. With the Lemons to Lemonade strategy, (a) Butler could choose not to march and the Task Force would not receive any funds to promote diversity education programs; (b) Butler's march could be short, and the Task Force would raise a minimal amount of funding; and (c) Butler's march could last a long time, in which case the longer the march lasted, the more funds that would be raised for human rights education. The Lemons to Lemonade campaign began in January prior to the Aryan Nations march in July. Individuals and organizations were asked to (a) sign a petition in support of human rights and (b) join the pledge drive to raise funds for human rights education by committing a self-determined amount per minutes for the duration of the march. People could also select the specific human rights group(s) to receive their pledge (Hult, 2011). May 28 saw the delivery of a human rights seminar for hundreds of high school students from northern Idaho, organized by northern Idaho regional *Spokesman-Review* editor Ken Sands. The *Spokesman-Review* and the KCTFHR sponsored high school students from Seattle to be the speakers/presenters at the seminar. The seminar was part of a larger initiative that included a series run by the newspaper from May 29 through July 13, 1998. The *Spokesman-Review* produced 130,000 "In It Together" posters to be displayed in cars and homes, along with an eight-week in-depth newspaper series titled "In It Together." The newspaper used 10 reporters, three editorial writers, three photographers, and five additional staff for the series. All 28 articles and letters were later compiled and published together (KCTFHR History, n.d.).

The KCTFHR funded extensive advertising campaigns including "Idaho Is For Everyone" posters, "Idaho Human Rights" billboards, brochures, newspaper adds, and so on. During the Aryan Nations Coeur d'Alene march in 1998, numerous businesses in Kootenai County used their marques that weekend to register their support for human rights. Marshall Mend, a founding member of the KCTFHR and local realtor, organized all these advertising projects (KCTFHR History, n.d.).

© wellphoto/Shutterstock.com

On July 11, 1998, the KCTFHR joined various groups from Washington and Idaho at the Idaho and Washington border for a "Hands Across the Border for Human Rights" press conference where they presented a list of events they would host on Saturday and Sunday, July 18 and 19 (Hands Across the Border for Human Rights July 18, 1998, 2019). The events were endorsed by a number of Republican and Democratic members of Congress and state legislators from Washington and Idaho. The list of supporters also included county commissioners, mayors, chambers of commerce and state office holders including Idaho Governor Phil Batt.

On July 18, Richard Butler and his Aryan Nations marched for 27 minutes on Sherman Avenue, the main street in Coeur d'Alene. Butler wanted the Task Force to come and heckle him and his supporters and labeled the Task Force members as cowards when they refused to do so. The Lemons to Lemonade counter response that had been initiated beginning in January by the KCTFHR gave community members a way to voice their opposition to the hate message and march by pledging donations to human rights organizations for each minute the Aryan Nations marched. A total of $35,484.96 was raised (Anti-Hate Drive Exceeds $35,000, 1998, p. 1). Of the funds raised, donors designated $10,000 to several specific human rights organizations including the Spokane Chapter of the NAACP and the Seattle based NWCAMH. The task force divided the remaining $24,000 into three grant periods over a year for public school teachers to use on programs and materials to promote diversity (Hult, 2011). By announcing the awards at three separate times throughout the year, the Task Force garnered greater publicity for their strategic success over the Aryan Nations. By the day of the march, 2,753 petition signatures had been collected, of which 2,526 chose to pledge funds (T. Stewart, personal communication, August 19, 2019). Grants were awarded to groups including the North Idaho College Equality Club, the Gonzaga University Institute for Action Against Hate, Rebecca's Awesome Kids—Post Falls, Tom Hunter's proposal to use music to celebrate human rights, and many others (T. Stewart, personal communication, August 19, 2019). All grants were for programs and educational materials to assist lessons in diversity. The Lemons to Lemonade campaign was borrowed from the residents of Boyertown, Pennsylvania, who used this idea in response to a KKK rally (KCTFHR History, n.d.).

Instead of attending the Aryan Nations march in Coeur d'Alene on July 18, KCTFHR along with many civic and human rights organizations and individuals from Idaho and Washington held a counterrally with their human rights partners in Spokane, Washington—an hour away from the Aryan Nations march. An Idaho motorcade decorated with orange ribbons and signs met with over more than 1,000 people on the campus of Gonzaga University (T. Stewart, personal communication, August 19, 2019). Many businesses in Kootenai County on that Saturday offered several hours of free recreation (e.g., bowling centers, theaters, skate plazas, and go cart fun).

On July 19th, interfaith groups held a service at St. Pius X Catholic Church in Coeur d'Alene with 700 in attendance for the speakers, music, prayers, and readings from both Washington and Idaho as well as a joint Spokane/Coeur d'Alene Choir performance. At the end of the weekend, Tony Stewart on behalf of the KCTFHR declared "This sends a strong message across the United States that the people of the Inland Northwest reject a message of prejudice and bigotry" (T. Stewart, personal communication, August 19, 2019).

Since 1998, the KCTFHR has sponsored an annual human rights banquet in Coeur d'Alene. A portion of the profits go to four minority scholarships at North Idaho College in partnership with the North Idaho College Foundation. The highlight of each year's banquet program is the keynote speaker.

POINTS TO PONDER

How was the Lemons to Lemonade campaign a win-win situation for the KCTFHR? Could this be a strategy you could use in your community to discourage demonstrations of hate?

1999: RALLY TO CELEBRATE HUMAN RIGHTS FOR ALL PEOPLE

In early 1999, the Aryan Nations under the leadership of Richard Butler once again applied for a parade permit from the city of Coeur d'Alene to be held downtown on July 10, 1999 as a follow up to their 1998 march (Struck, 2017). Upon hearing of the permit request, the KCTFHR at their monthly meeting elected to counter the march with a rally at the North Idaho College Schuler Auditorium on the same date and at the same time as the march. Hundreds of area residents representing the diversity of the region attended the two-hour program featuring a keynote by Idaho Governor Dirk Kempthorne along with speeches by several other regional leaders and musical performances.

> Governor Kempthorne denounced the neo-Nazi march when he declared: "The idea that this soil is now used as a verbal battleground for hatred and the display of Swastikas is not Idaho. What's happening here today in this auditorium is Idaho."

> The Governor's address was followed by North Idaho College President Michael Burke who said: "Unfortunately, it only takes one incident to remind us that progress in human rights can sometimes be glacial. We're not there yet. We remain a house divided against itself"

> Jeanne Givens, a member of the Coeur d'Alene Tribe and former Idaho State Representative, spoke of the true meaning of human rights to the gathered crowd with the words: "Human rights is not about a parade permit. Human Rights is how we act. It's how we walk the talk."

> Doug Cresswell, president of the KCTFHR, spoke for the Task Force as the sponsor of the event with words of encouragement: "This is the right place to be. This is what we should be doing this morning—celebrating human rights for all people"

> The KCTFHR distributed buttons to the attendees with the words: "Not in Our Town . . . the Northwest is Too Great for Hate." A large banner was hung reading: THE RIGHT TO MARCH DOES NOT MAKE THE MARCH RIGHT (T. Stewart, personal communication, August 19, 2019).

Once again, the KCTFHR executed a successful plan for citizens to have an alternative event to lift their voices in opposition to those who preach hate and also gave the media the opportunity to report the KCTFHR message.

In the Fall of 1999, another mailing of 5,000 copies of a 16-page booklet with a glossy timeline to residents of Bonner County area depicting a message of racial and religious hatred (Lalley, 1999). The BCHRTF lead a peaceful campaign of opposition to the 11th Hour Remnant Messenger by holding rallies, human rights events, working with schools promoting human rights curriculum, close communication with local law enforcement, media campaigns, and coordination with political leaders (Geranios, 1998). The hate group had left Idaho by the early 21st Century.

DISCUSSION QUESTIONS

1.

Briefly describe the situation in the case. What aspects of your description are judgments (value statements about what is good or bad) and what aspects are objective statements?

2.

What were specific strategies the Kootenai County Task Force on Human Relations (KCTFHR) implemented to prevent the success of hate groups in the community? Were these successful? Could they be used today?

3.

What role did education play for the task force? Why are these strategies important and how can they be used today?

4.

What goal(s) can you envision for the outcomes in this case? Brainstorm new strategies for reaching the goal(s). What are the strengths and limitations of each?

5.

What lessons do you take away from this case and how might you apply them in your own context?

REFERENCES

About KCTFHR. (n.d.). Retrieved March 2, 2020, from www.idahohumanrights. org, https://www.idahohumanrights.org/about.html

Anti-Hate Drive Exceeds $35,000. (1998, August 3). *The Seattle Times*. Retrieved March 3, 2020, from archive.seattletimes.com, https://archive.seattletimes.com/ archive/?date=19980803&slug=2764566

Associated Press. (1986, October 7). Man tied to white supremacists faces charges in Idaho bombings. *The New York Times*. Retrieved from https://www.nytimes. com/1986/10/07/us/man-tied-to-white-supremacists-faces-charges-in-idaho-bombings.html

Coeur d'Alene Tribe and North Idaho College 9 Point Agreement. (2018, October). Retrieved from https://www.nic.edu/about/9PointAgreement.pdf

Geranios, K. N. (1998, December 20). Wealthy backers of white supremacists raise concerns in Idaho. *Los Angeles Times*. Retrieved from Los Angeles Times. https://www. latimes.com/archives/la-xpm-1998-dec-20-me-55819-story.html

Hammond, B. (2015, November 27). A brief history of human rights in Bonner County. *Sandpoint Reader*. Retrieved April 15, 2020, from Sandpoint Reader. https:// sandpointreader.com/a-brief-history-of-human-rights-in-bonner-county/

Hands Across the Border for Human Rights July 18, 1998. (2019). [YouTube Video]. In *YouTube*. Retrieved from https://www.youtube.com/watch?v=lfEFobUiMGw&t= 1374s

Hult, K. (2011, September 11). *Fig Tree—Kootenai County task force on human relations marks 30 years of efforts to overcome hate in Inland Northwest*. Retrieved from http://www. thefigtree.org/sept11/090711KootenaiTFHR.html

Hult, K. (2016, May 16). *Fig Tree Kootenai County task force on human relations member, Marshal Mend, reflects on work*. Retrieved March 2, 2020, from www.thefigtree. org, https://www.thefigtree.org/may16/050116kctfhrmend.html

KCTFHR History. (n.d.). Retrieved from www.idahohumanrights.org, https://www. idahohumanrights.org/history.html

Keating, K. B. (1995, May 15). Racist plans move to North Idaho Ex-Kkk leader is considered one of Nation's most active and most dangerous militants. *The Spokesman-Review*. Retrieved March 3, 2020, from www.spokesman.com, https://www.spokesman. com/stories/1995/may/15/racist-plans-move-to-north-idaho-ex-kkk-leader-is/

Lalley, H. (1999, October 17). *Hate mail delivered to Sandpoint*. Retrieved March 3, 2020, from culteducation.com, https://culteducation.com/group/871-christian-identity/3698-hate-mail-delivered-to-sandpoint.html

McAlister, G. (n.d.). *LibGuides: Human rights collection: Home*. Retrieved March 2, 2020, from nic.libguides.com, https://nic.libguides.com/HumanRights

McCary, D. (2006, June, 12). *Robert Jay Mathews, founder of the white-supremacist group The Order, is killed during an FBI siege on Whidbey Island on December 8, 1984*. Retrieved March 2, 2020, from www.historylink.org, https://www.historylink.org/File/7921

Morlin, B., & White, J. S. (1996, October 9). Bombing suspects arrested three suspected in Spokane valley robberies, terrorism. *The Spokesman-Review*. Retrieved March 3, 2020, from www.spokesman.com, https://www.spokesman.com/stories/1996/oct/09/bombing-suspects-arrested-three-suspected-in/

Not in Our Town. (n.d.). *Kootenai county task force on human relations*. Retrieved April 15, 2020, from www.niot.org, https://www.niot.org/group/kootenai-county-task-force-human-relations

Pankaatz, H. (2010, August 17). *Neo-Nazi who shot Denver radio host Alan Berg dies in federal prison in Pa*. Retrieved March 2, 2020, from The Denver Post. https://www.denverpost.com/2010/08/17/neo-nazi-who-shot-denver-radio-host-alan-berg-dies-in-federal-prison-in-pa/

Powers, K. (2011). *When Hate inhabits space: The Aryan Nation's use of free space in Idaho and the state's refusal to be defined by the White power Movement*. University of Puget Sound. Retrieved from https://www.pugetsound.edu/files/resources/7908_2011KathleenPowers.pdf

Smith, L. (2017, November 6). *This brash Jewish radio host was murdered by white supremacists for denouncing anti-Semitism*. Retrieved March 2, 2020, from Medium. https://timeline.com/alan-berg-jewish-murder-denver-57f54b2989dd

Stewart, T., & Gissel, N. (n.d.). *Democracy as counter to hate groups*. Retrieved April 15, 2020, from Not in Our Town. https://www.niot.org/action-hub/local-lessons/democracy-counter-hate-groups

Struck, D. (2017, August 31). The Idaho town that stared down hate—and won. *The Christian Science Monitor*. Retrieved April 15, 2020, from Christian Science Monitor, https://www.csmonitor.com/USA/Society/2017/0831/The-Idaho-town-that-stared-down-hate-and-won

U.S. Department of Justice. (1985). *Annal report of the attorney general of the United States.* Retrieved from https://www.ncjrs.gov/pdffiles1/Digitization/103953NCJRS.pdf

Walkin, D. (2004, September 9). Richard G. Butler, 86, founder of the Aryan Nations, dies. *The New York Times.* Retrieved from https://www.nytimes.com/2004/09/09/us/richard-g-butler-86-founder-of-the-aryan-nations-dies.html

Wassmuth, B., & Bryant, M. J. (2002). Not in our world: A perspective of community organizing against hate. *Journal of Hate Studies*, 1(1), 109–131. https://doi.org/10.33972/jhs.4

Woo, E. (2002, August 31). *Bill Wassmuth, 61; Ex-Priest led anti-hate group, helped to bankrupt Aryan Nations.* Retrieved March 3, 2020, from Los Angeles Times. https://www.latimes.com/archives/la-xpm-2002-aug-31-me-wassmuth31-story.html

Chapter 3

THE STORY IN IDAHO
(2000–2020)

© Olinchuk/Shutterstock.com

OVERVIEW

Local community members created the Kootenai County Task Force on Human Relations (KCTFHR) in 1981, adopting a nonconfrontational approach that focused on victim support, opposing discrimination, organizing counter events during hate group activities, promoting state and federal human rights legislation, and coordinating educational programs and community events to advance human rights (KCTFHR, n.d.a). The original motivation to found the KCTFHR was rooted in opposition to the work of Richard Butler, founder of the Aryan Nations and the Church of Jesus Christ Christian, after he purchased land for a compound in 1973 in Hayden, Idaho (Guilhem, 2017) and his followers began a spree of hate crimes and harassment that lasted for several decades. The KCTFHR is recognized in partnership with the Southern Poverty Law Center for bankrupting the Aryan Nations in 2000 by winning a $6.3 million civil judgment. The KCTHFR has continued their work for more than four decades after their founding. "We have learned that we can't be silent when these things take place." Stewart said (Hult, 2011).

Timeline

1981	Founding of the Kootenai County Task Force on Human Relations (Coeur d'Alene, Countering hate graffiti and harassment)
2000, August to September	*Keenan v. Aryan Nations* Civil Trial (Coeur d'Alene, Countering a physical hate attack)
2009, August	Hands Across the Border, Part II (Washington/Idaho state line, Countering the hate fliers)
2010, October	Rally for Freedom, Equality, and Justice, with Fundraising for Targeted Communities (Coeur d'Alene, Countering a hate rally)
2012	Environmental and Health Accountability and Elections as Evidence of Community Values (Bonner County, Countering a new hate compound and candidate for sheriff)
2017, September	Proclaiming Love Lives Here and Granting Scholarships When Others Promote Hate (Sandpoint and Bonner County, Countering hate fliers)
2017, October	Encouraging Belonging (Boise State University, countering hate on campus

1981: FOUNDING OF THE KOOTENAI COUNTY TASK FORCE ON HUMAN RELATIONS

The KCTFHR is recognized, in partnership with the Southern Poverty Law Center, for bankrupting the Aryan Nations in 2000 by winning a $6.3 million civil judgment, forcing the sale of the compound to the Gregory C. Carr Foundation, turned into a peace park and gifted to the North Idaho College Foundation. The property was sold in 2020 with proceeds endowing the Gregory C. Carr Chair for Human Rights at North Idaho College (Associated Press, 2019a). The KCTHFR has continued their work for more than four decades after their founding, with proactive and reactive responses to hate and advising other communities that are challenged by hate groups, providing nonviolent resources and peaceful strategies that have stood the test of time. "We have learned that we can't be silent when these things take place. It's all about control," Stewart said. "Who determines it? We can let them control our behavior, or we can control it" (Hult, 2011).

Twenty-one people serve on the KCTFHR board. Nine seats are open while 12 seats are held for representatives of the Coeur d'Alene Tribe; Hispanic/Latino, Asian American, Jewish and African American communities; local governments in Kootenai County; the Coeur d'Alene Chamber of Commerce; religious, law enforcement, gay-lesbian-bisexual-transvestite groups; the North Idaho College student; and education communities. All on the task force volunteer their time (Hult, 2011).

As of this writing, Tony Stewart and Marshall Mend are founding members who continue to be active on the board even after having received death threats over their years of service. At one time, road barriers were defaced with swastikas and the words, "Kill Marshall Mend." Through the years, the KCTFHR remains committed to promoting legislation and public policy that advances human and civil rights, opposing discrimination or the denial of equal protection of the laws based upon race, color, religion, creed, gender, age, disability, national origin, or sexual orientation, celebrating diversity, and supporting victims of malicious harassment (Hult, 2016).

2000: *KEENAN V. ARYAN NATIONS* CIVIL TRIAL

On July 1, 1998, Victoria Keenan was driving her small honeybee car on a quiet Idaho state highway that fronted the Aryan Nations compound. She was accompanied by her19-year-old son, Jason. The two were headed home after attending a wedding (Southern Law Poverty Center, Keenan V, Aryan Nation, n.d.).

Tensions were extremely high in the region because of the plans for an upcoming Aryan Nations march in Coeur d'Alene later that month. While passing the entrance to the Aryan Nations headquarters, the Keenan's car backfired and Aryan Nations security guards Jesse Warfield, John Yeager, and Shane Wright (who were under the influence of beer), believed that members of the Jewish community were invading the compound (ABC News, 2006).

The three guards got into a truck and carried high-powered weapons. They located the Keenan's car and chased it for two miles down the rural state highway. The guards fired at the car, hitting it five times, and ran the car off the highway. They struck Victoria Keenan with the butt of a gun and pulled her by the hair while her son was menaced by the guards who then yelled at the victims "Don't f . . . with the Aryans." The attack ended when a nearby homeowner approached carrying a weapon (Balch, 2006).

Several days later, Ms. Keenan contacted Tony Stewart who convinced her to meet with the Task Force's attorney Norm Gissel. Gissel became the Keenan family's attorney and after several weeks working with Victoria, Gissel contacted Morris Dees of the Southern Poverty Law Center. Dees agreed to take the case and his legal team worked on the case for two years, assisted by Norm Gissel and Ken Howard, the latter was a prominent Idaho civil attorney specializing in tort cases (Deshais, 2019).

The trial took place in the Idaho First Judicial District Court in Coeur d'Alene and drew national and international media attention due to the Southern Poverty Law Center and Dees heading the plaintiff's team. Dees had a history of winning numerous civil cases securing millions of dollars in damages for their clients who had been assaulted or killed by violent members of hate groups operating across America. The trial opened on Monday, August 28, 2000 before a 12-member jury with the jury reaching a verdict on Thursday,

September 7, 2000. They jury unanimously awarded $6.3 million in damages to Keenan, against the Aryan Nations, Richard Butler, and the three security guards. The award bankrupted the Aryan Nations and Richard Butler (ABC News, 2006).

After U.S. Bankruptcy Court case no. 0021265 auction, the property was awarded to Keenan. They sold the property to Idaho native and philanthropist Greg Carr for $250,000 who in turn destroyed the compound, named it a peace park and deeded the 20-accre piece of property to the North Idaho College Foundation in 2002 (KCTFHR History, n.d.).

2000 TO 2003: FUNDRAISING, RECOGNITION, AND EDUCATION FOR HUMAN RIGHTS

Since 2000, the KCTFHR has been the recipient of the Coeur d'Alene and Lake City high schools' annual student human rights fundraising campaign. The proceeds from this fundraiser are presented to the KCTFHR at the annual Coeur d'Alene and Lake City men's basketball game featuring a fun competition known as the "Fight for the Fish" trophy. The KCTFHR receives more than $1,000 per year from this student fundraiser (KCTFHR History, n.d.).

The KCTFHR established the Human Rights Education Institute (HREI) in 1998. On September 15 and 16, 2000, North Idaho College and HREI cosponsored a two-day symposium for 300 Idaho and Washington educators titled "Celebrating Diversity in the Classroom." The HREI appropriated $10,000 for the conference so that there would be no conference fee charged to teachers attending the event. Prominent educators from across the United States presented at the conference. North Idaho College president Michael Burke welcomed and addressed the conference attendees (KCTFHR History, n.d.).

The Gregory C. Carr Foundation in January 2002 awarded a $1,000,000 gift to the HREI in Coeur d'Alene as seed money for the establishment of a human rights center and program in Coeur d'Alene, Idaho (KCTFHR History, n.d.).

During March 22 to 29, 2003, the North Idaho College Popcorn Forum Lecture Series and the Gonzaga University Institute for Action Against Hate along with 11 other colleges hosted a nine-day symposium titled "Confronting Hate: Humanity's Greatest Challenge." The nine-day series was located on both college campuses. Members of the KCTFHR were key organizers/partners in the series (KCTFHR History, n.d.).

POINTS TO PONDER

Think about the significance of the Keenan's winning their trial against the Aryan Nations and the impact it had on the surrounding community. Why was this effective? And what did this decision symbolize for the future of the community?

2006 TO 2009: DOCUMENTARY, COUNSELING, AND A TRUSTEE CAMPAIGN

From January through March, 2006, a 10-week television documentary titled "Special Series: Celebrating the 25-year history of the Kootenai County Task Force on Human Relations" was broadcast for the first time on KSPS PBS TV and later on Idaho Public Television. Also on January 12, 2006, the Kootenai County Task Force on Human Relations partnered with the Post Falls and Coeur d'Alene school districts to host the 21st annual Dr., Martin Luther King, Jr. Fifth-Grade Student's Program with an inspiring message from Billy Mills, the 1964 Olympic Gold Medalist runner. His appearance was especially inspiring to minority students as he related how he had overcome prejudice directed at him as a minority individual himself. On March 21, the KCTFHR held the 9th annual human rights banquet with Mississippi Attorney General Jim Hood who shared how he had successfully prosecuted one of the men who had many years ago participated in the murder of the three civil rights workers in Philadelphia, Mississippi. Later during the month of November, KCTFHR partnered with sister organization the HREI, to host the Ann Frank Photo Exhibit at the HREI Center. Hundreds of school children visited the exhibit that month.

It unfortunately was also a year that saw a number of activities under the umbrella of prejudice and bigotry. After a night of drinking on July 15, two young men set fire to a small cross on the lawn of a biracial family in Spirit Lake, Idaho. The KCTFHR was part of negotiations that lead to the young men pleading guilty to a misdemeanor, with one of the young men agreeing to counseling with three members of the KCTFHR Board; he later joined the U.S. Navy.

Stan Hess, a neo-Nazi, who had been listed by the Southern Poverty Law Center as one of the 100 most prolific White supremacists in the United States, ran in the general election for a seat on the North Idaho College Board of Trustees in November, 2006. The KCTFHR, along with 150 additional community leaders, opposed his candidacy with newspaper advertisements titled "Speak Out for Human Rights" and the area newspapers ran editorials opposing Hess' candidacy. Hess was defeated in a landslide.

In 2007, the KCTFHR members continued to speak out for human rights, whether they were being respected or ridiculed. A founding KCTFHR member joined five other Pacific Northwest leaders for a six-month in-depth series by The *Spokesman-Review* newspaper titled "Leadership Dialogues." During a speech at HREI, three White supremacists interrupted Stewart. The White supremacists left and Stewart continued his speech without incident.

The 11th annual human rights banquet in the spring of 2008 featuring human rights philanthropist Gregory Carr, who had purchased and destroyed the Aryan Nations Compound after acquiring it from the Keenan in the 2000 civil trial. It was also the year that both the weekly North Idaho College TV Public Forum PBS series and the North Idaho College (NIC) Popcorn Forum lecture series ended with the retirement of NIC Political Science faculty member and producer of both the TV and lecture series. Over 27 years, the Task Force had enjoyed the opportunity to be guests, to be visible in the community, and to make sure that the message of human rights was heard over and over again for all those listening to those venues. Significantly, North Idaho College became the repository of the KCTFHR's papers, videos, and all other documents, providing a rich collection of research materials available to the public.

The work of the KCTFHR in 2009 included their yearly programs, the 24th annual Dr. Martin Luther King, Jr. Children's Program in January, the 12th annual

© wideonet/Shutterstock.com

human rights banquet in March featuring keynoter Nontombi Naomi Tutu, daughter of South Africa Archbishop Desmond Tutu, and the August North Idaho Fair booth. However, in the summer of 2009, White separatists' Paul R. Mullet, Kevin McGurre, and Todd Weston were seen distributing racist flyers in the yards of citizens in the Washington cities of Spokane, Spokane Valley, and Liberty Lake and in the Idaho cities and towns of Coeur d'Alene, Post Falls, Spirit Lake, Dalton Gardens, and Sandpoint (Racist flyers distributed in Spokane Valley, n.d.).

A "Hands Across the Border" press conference and rally were organized for a second time on August 21, 2009, the first time had been in 1998. Hate fliers were being distributed throughout the region (KHQ, 2009), the KCTFHR brought together 19 speakers from the region's government and law enforcement officials, including the head of law enforcement for the Coeur d'Alene Tribe to meet at the Washington/Idaho border (KCTFHR History, n.d.). Master of Ceremonies and cofounder of the KCTFHR Tony Stewart, began the press conference with the warning: "We reject the hate and will aggressively prosecute all hate crimes" (T. Stewart, personal communication, August 19, 2019).

Also in 2009, three brothers (Frank, Ira, and William Tankovich) arrived in Coeur d'Alene, Idaho from California and began to seriously threaten a local Hispanic family. The KCTFHR attorney, Norm Gissel, provided support for the victims and in late 2010 the brothers were convicted under Idaho's

Malicious Harassment statue. One brother was returned to California to face a murder charge with the other two brothers eventually assigned by an Idaho judge to work at the HREI Center for a year of community service.

On September 7, 2010, the KCTFHR hosted a public celebration on the grounds of the Kootenai County Courthouse to commemorate the 10th anniversary of the *"Keenan v. Aryan Nations"* civil trial. Speakers included the Keenan's attorneys Norm Gissel and Ken Howard, philanthropist Greg Carr, Coeur d'Alene Mayor Sandi Bloem, Kootenai County Commission Chair Rick Currie, and Coeur d'Alene Tribal Council Vice-Chair Ernie Stensgar (KCTFHR History, n.d).

2010: SUPPORTING COMMUNITIES REGIONALLY AND FUNDRAISING FOR TARGETED COMMUNITIES

After Butler's compound, the location of the Aryan Nations headquarters and Church of Jesus Christ Christian, was destroyed in 2001 and Butler died in 2004, his estimated 200 followers dispersed to Florida, Alabama, Pennsylvania, upstate New York, and the Midwest, according to Gissel, KCTFHR attorney (Cockle & Oregonian, 2012). However, people were also still trying to carry on Butler's work in the Inland Northwest. Paul R. Mullet of Athol took steps to relocate the Aryan Nations headquarters to John Day (Grant County), Oregon, attracted to the rural terrain for survivalist training. In February of 2010, the KCTFHR was asked to assist the John Day community. KCTFHR members Tony Stewart and Norm Gissel, along with Diana Gissel were central to community rallies and speeches held on February 26. On April 30, Stewart and Norm Gissel were also asked to work with the Townsend, Montana community in response to racists activities there.

During the summer of 2010, members of the Westboro Baptist Church (WBC), an anti-lesbian, gay, bisexual, and transgender (LGBT) group out of Topeka, Kansas, announced its members would travel to Coeur d'Alene, Idaho to protest. The protest was against North Idaho College's Fall theater stage production of the "Laramie Project," a play about the murder of Matthew Shepard, a gay student in Wyoming (Bindel, 2014).

Based on past experiences with similar threats from hate groups, the KCTFHR began exploring alternative strategies to address the WBC's offensive and divisive message that included thanking God for the death of American soldiers and celebrating breast cancer as God's punishment for acceptance of homosexuality. The WBC protested first at several locations in Spokane, Washington. On the morning of October 22, 2010, the day after the Spokane protests, the WBC held a rally on the North Idaho College campus from 8:00 a.m. until 8:30 a.m. (Graman, 2010).

© igorstevanovic/Shutterstock.com

The KCTFHR purposely scheduled a human rights unity rally immediately following the church protest at the HREI adjacent to the college (About Human Rights Education Institute, n.d.). This gave the media an opportunity to attend both the WBC and KCTFHR events, while asking the community to only attend the KCTFHR counterrally.

A crowd of hundreds filled the main hall for the counterrally with an overflow crowd in the parking lot to listen to 18 speakers from Idaho and Washington declare their support for freedom, equality, and justice. The speakers represented all segments of society. Messages of support were received from the presidents of Washington State University, the University of Idaho, Gonzaga University, Whitworth University, Eastern Washington University, Lewis-Clark State College, and North Idaho College. Audience members wore yellow ribbons to honor military men and women who have served or are serving in the armed services (Stewart & Gissel, 2012).

Realizing that the anti-gay message of the WBC at North Idaho College was both offensive and hurtful to the members of the North Idaho College's Gay and Straight Alliance (GSA), the audience at the unity rally raised over $300 for the GSA club (North Idaho College Sentinel, n.d.).

Of note the following year, the KCTFHR's 14th annual human rights banquet hosted keynote speaker Arun Gandhi, the grandson of Mohandas Gandhi, at the sold-out banquet. Another important KCTFHR milestone for the year was support to establish the Benewah County Human Rights Task Force, located in St. Maris, Idaho. The new group would become a major contributor to assist the public schools of Benewah County in diversity and human rights programs. Also in 2011, the Northwest Coalition for Human Rights, a new organization devoted to combating hate in the Inland Northwest was formed. The Northwest Coalition Against Malicious Harassment, later renamed the Northwest Coalition for Human Dignity had disbanded due to financial constraints in 2003. The need for coordinated efforts, collaboration, and a communication network in the Inland Northwest were evident, and the new organization was created to "facilitate connections and communication among organizations and individuals who are engaged in human rights and social justice work in the Northwest," according to the coalition's newsletter and website (NW Coalition for Human Rights—Working for social justice and equality in the Pacific Northwest, n.d.).

2012: ENVIRONMENTAL AND HEALTH ACCOUNTABILITY AND ELECTIONS AS EVIDENCE OF COMMUNITY VALUES

HEADLINE

20 years after Ruby Ridge siege, extremists are fewer in northern Idaho but still remain - oregonlive.com

On March 12, 2011, Shawn Winkler, a 33-year-old native of York, Pennsylvania, purchased 17.3 acres in the Hoodoo Mountains of Bonner County, Idaho. Information about the purchase was available through the deed of trust filed in Bonner County public records and interviews given by the seller. The property was advertised for sale in the local newspaper and was sold for $72,000, with a $3,000 down payment. The site was relatively close to the former Aryan Nations "world headquarters" in Kootenai County and Winkler had a vision for families affiliated with the Klan or Aryan Nations to build homes on the site (Spokesman ReviewCenter, 2012). In an interview with the *lentellignce Report, Winkler referenced his property as a replacement for the Butler compound, providing a home for Aryan Nations gatherings.* "You ought to see what we're doing up there, so you can compare it to what Pastor Butler had going back in the day down at the Aryan Nations." Winkler faced challenges over illegal logging and sewage disposal, a building location permit required by state law that was not acquired, and $750 monthly property payments delinquencies (Southern Poverty Law Center, 2012). Winkler lost the property.

On January 13, the KCTFHR organized its 27th annual Dr. Martin Luther King, Jr. Children's Program featuring a live performance by the well-known theater company "Living Voices" out of Seattle, Washington. The fifth-grade students were taught about the historical human rights struggles in the South during the civil rights movement of the 1960s through the medium of live theater. As the students left on buses from the North Idaho College campus, they saw bigotry up close as Shaun Winkler and his followers were gathered on the sidewalk with signs depicting racist messages along with a display of the Confederate flag.

HEADLINE

Neo-Nazi Builds North Idaho Compound to Replace Defunct Aryan Nations | Southern Poverty Law Center

In March 2012, Winkler filed as a Republican candidate to run for sheriff of Bonner County, Idaho. In an article in the *Bonner County Daily Bee, Winkler was quoted as saying* "Most people don't know that we don't just oppose the Jews and the Negroes. We also oppose sexual predators and drugs of any kind." Winkler said he believed perpetrators of sex crimes "should be hung immediately." Winkler also said "I have no hate toward anyone" (Southern Poverty Law Center, Neo-Nazi Builds North Idaho Compound to Replace Defunct Aryan Nations, 2012).

Winkler invited McKnight, a reporter, to a barbecue, a Christian Identity-style church service and cross burning at the HooDoo site in early May just before the elections. When McKnight went to the gathering, he was greeted by Mark Eliseuson dressed in a Ku Klux Klan (KKK) robe and holding a rifle. The church service included praise for Adolf Hitler. Winkler went on to say that he was being encouraged to build a "double-block wall" to protect his compound, referencing Ruby Ridge. "I said, 'What? We ain't planning on having a war right here.' People seem to think that just because we're in the right-wing movement that we have this weird philosophy and this kind of activity is going to happen. I'm not saying it won't." Winkler told those present, "We're messengers, and Pastor Butler said the same thing. We don't carry out deeds unless we feel the Holy Spirit moves us to do so. We're generally a legal organization." Winkler told McKnight that he (Winkler) was the leader of a klavern, or local chapter, of the Knights of the KKK—the same Klan faction that was founded in 1975 by David Duke (MorlinCenter, 2012).

McKnight's story about the racist sheriff candidate was published in the local paper, the *Bonner County Daily Bee*, where reporter Cameron Rasmusson said many readers were angry about the coverage because it was bad for the community's reputation. When the election was held, Winkler finished last in the three-way race for sheriff, with only 182 votes.

Within a week of losing the election, Winkler and several followers were in Coeur d'Alene, carrying signs and picketing outside Atilano's Mexican restaurant. "They don't want us to be here," said Gonzales, and Atilano's employee. "They want Coeur d'Alene to be white" (Cockle & Oregonian, 2012).

POINTS TO PONDER

If you were in the community's shoes, would you want this story to be publicized? What would be the pros and cons to having this story being released?

Protestors and counter-protesters engaged with each other and police officers were called to the scene, backed up by six Kootenai County sheriff's deputies and four Idaho State Police troopers, according to police reports. Police reports indicated that a person at the scene was verbally confronted by Winkler, who called her a "retarded Hispanic c__t" who "needed to leave his town because she was not welcome, and that she wasn't dead yet." The city prosecutors did not press charges against Winkler (Southern Law Poverty Center, Neo-Nazi Builds North Idaho Compound to Replace Defunct Aryan Nations, 2012).

Brenda Hammond, president of the Bonner County Human Rights Task Force, said "The task force agrees that the best way to deal with these elements in our society is to bring them out into the light. We don't need to sensationalize their actions, but we definitely need to respond—lest our silence be interpreted as acceptance" (Southern Law Poverty Center, Neo-Nazi Builds North Idaho Compound to Replace Defunct Aryan Nations, 2012).

2013 TO 2016: CREATING HUMAN RIGHTS LEGISLATION, ANTI-BULLYING EDUCATION, AND REGIONAL SUPPORT

On February 4, 2013, the KCTFHR initiated a proposed anti-discrimination ordinance prohibiting discrimination in housing, employment, and public accommodations on the basis of sexual orientation or gender identity/expression and presented the plan to the City of Coeur d'Alene Council. The KCTFHR drafted a letter to Mayor Sandi Bloem, stating in part "The City of Coeur d'Alene has the opportunity to move forward in advancing the principles we all have promoted for decades. We urge you to stand on the broad shoulders of those who have gone before you in confirming once again the dignity and rights of all our residents and share in this noble legacy" (T. Stewart, personal communication, August 19, 2019).

Following both the General Service's Committee and Council hearings with presentations led by the KCTFHR, the anti-discrimination ordinance was adopted by the Coeur d'Alene City Council on a five to one vote on June 4, 2013 (KCTFHR History, n.d.). Mayor Sandi Bloem and Council President Mike Kennedy were the key players in the adoption of the anti-discrimination ordinance. On June 6, "The *Spokesman-Review*" editorial read "Thus, the Lake City struck another blow for human rights, just as it did with its resistance to the White supremacists who tried to turn this scenic enclave into their ugly bunker of hate" (*Spokesman-Review*, 2013).

In the summer of 2013, Tony Stewart was a guest lecturer in six Coeur d'Alene high school classes where he learned of a serious pattern of bullying that had led to one of the school's students committing suicide the prior year. He and KCTFHR president Christie Wood met with the school district's superintendent to address the issue. Stewart was given permission to conduct a nationwide search for an anti-bullying expert to assist the school district's bullying problem. The search resulted in the selection of Steve Wessler, a former Maine Assistant Attorney General and former Director of the Portland, Maine based Center for Preventing Hate.

On September 25, 2013, the KCTFHR, Coeur d'Alene Tribe and the Kootenai Electric Utility Foundation presented funding at a press conference to the Coeur d'Alene School District for the implementation of an extensive long-range student-centered anti-bullying system for the school district. After four years, the results have shown a remarkable decrease in bullying in the schools (KCTFHR History, n.d.).

On October 8, 2013, Norm Gissel and Tony Stewart represented the KCTFHR along with cofounder Morris Dees of the Southern Poverty Law Center on a panel at the University of Idaho Law School discussing human and civil rights and strategies to combat hate.

During the Idaho Legislature's session in the spring of 2014, HB 426 and HB 427 were introduced with the intent to basically repeal all city ordinances in the state of Idaho that banned discrimination in housing, public accommodations, and employment based on sexual orientation. The KCTFHR joined other civil groups in Idaho, key business corporations, members of the public, and legislators supportive of human rights to kill the bills.

As a new proactive strategy, the KCTFHR created a parade entry in the Coeur d'Alene Chamber of Commerce American Heroes July 4th Parade. The entry won the clubs and organizations 1st Place Prize.

The year of 2014 also found the Coeur d'Alene Tribe once again being a target of hate when on Monday, July 14th a racist message was discovered scrawled on a Tribal historical marker. The KCTFHR responded immediately with a message to the Coeur d'Alene Tribe, to the public, and directly to the perpetrators(s) through a media release. Tony Stewart spoke for the KCTFHR saying "This is clearly a hate crime with the intent to promote anger and hatred directed at the Coeur d'Alene Tribe. It is unfortunately another example to remind us that we still have a challenge in eradicating racism from the world's society." Idaho Governor Butch Otter spoke of the incident in clear terms when he issued a statement that read in part: "This kind of hate-filled sentiment has no place in Idaho" (T. Stewart, personal communication, August 19, 2019).

In October 2014, Stewart represented KCTFHR during testimony before the Lewiston, Idaho City Council meeting where the Council was considering the adoption of an ordinance banning discrimination based on sexual orientation. On October 27, the Council approved the ordinance by a five to two vote.

The 18th annual KCTFHR human rights banquet was held on April 13, 2015 with Doug Echols, mayor of Rock Hill, South Carolina, sharing the story of how his city and a South Carolina court in January of that year vacated the 1961 conviction of nine young African American men for conducting a peaceful sit-in at a segregated lunch counter. Mayor Echols replayed the video of the dramatic court hearing for the banquet audience. It was an emotional moment for our banquet attendees.

In mid-August 2015, Stewart received a phone call from North Dakota University Dean of the College of Arts and Sciences, Debbie Storrs, requesting help from the KCTFHR regarding an ongoing community controversy that had risen in May when Usama Dakdok came to Grand Forks, North Dakota and delivered a public speech on "the dangers of Islam" that created serious tensions in the community and a counter protest. KCTFHR attorney Norm Gissel and Stewart visited the community over a three-day period on September 2 to 4, 2015, giving University of North Dakota (UND) class lectures, meetings with UND administrators, student groups on campus, the business community, and city leaders. They gave a public presentation at the St. Paul's Episcopal Church at the same hour of Mr. Dakdok's program.

There were no counter demonstrations or direct encounters between attendees at the two separate events.

On August 3, 2016, a reception was held at the HREI for the opening of the 138-piece KCTFHR exhibit titled "Coming Face to Face with Hate: A Search for a World Beyond Hate." The exhibit was on display at the Center for two months. On October 13, the KCTFHR partnered with North Idaho College to sponsor a daylong seminar titled "A Return to Civility in the Public Arena." Dr. Cornell W. Clayton, the Director of the Washington State University Thomas S Foley Institute for Public Policy, delivered the keynote address. The day seminar included presenters from the religious, business, political, and education communities.

In August 2017, three members of the KCTFHR were part of in-depth interviews with journalist Doug Struck regarding the history of our organization and the campaign to defeat the threats from the Aryan Nations. The interview was published on August 31 in the "*Christian Science Monitor*" under the heading "The Idaho Town that Stared Down Hate—and Won."

2017: PROCLAIMING LOVE LIVES HERE AND GRANTING SCHOLARSHIPS WHEN OTHERS PROMOTE HATE

From June until August 2017, Sandpoint and Bonner County residents were bombarded with vile hate-filled flyers from out-of-state hate groups with unidentified local helpers. A total of nine different flyers either targeted individuals or minority groups. One flyer depicted Sandpoint Mayor Shelby Rognstad in a gas chamber. Again, the Bonners County Human Rights Task Force (BCHRTF) in partnership with the KCTFHR rose to the occasion, united the community, and held a press conference on September 6, 2017. Idaho Governor Butch Otter and Idaho State Senator Shawn Keough sent strong messages condemning the hate. With extensive media present, speakers at the press conference included four members of the BCHRTF, three members of the KCTFHR, Sandpoint Mayor Shelby Rognstad, the CEO of the Sandpoint Chamber of Commerce, the superintendent of the local school district, and three ministers of local churches (Morlin, 2017Center). Stewart from the KCTFHR read a statement from Idaho

Governor Butch Otter that read in part "We have dealt with White Supremacists and other groups filled by hatred before. We told them then, as we continue to tell them now, and in no uncertain or ambiguous terms, they are not wanted here and will never be welcome here" (T. Stewart, personal communication, August 19, 2019).

Following the press conference, church leaders, local organizations, and individuals rallied in support of human rights with a number of diversity events and many Sandpoint residents displayed signs stating "Love Lives Here" as another example of how a community found nonviolent means to prevail over hate while advancing human rights and celebrating diversity (Healey, 2017).

The BCHRTF has continued to be a major force in the area promoting human rights, countering any activities based on a message of hate, support for victims and as the recipient of two major estate gifts the BCHRTF provided scholarships to college students.

2017: ENCOURAGING BELONGING

Dr. Jill Gill, professor of History at Boise State University (BSU), contacted Tony Stewart in the early summer of 2017, and invited Stewart and KCTFHR attorney Norm Gissel to be the keynote speakers for the inaugural symposium of the BSU Marilyn Shuler Human Rights Initiative on October 26, 2017 to be held in the Simplot Ballroom (Boise State News, 2017).

In correspondence with Stewart over several months, Dr. Gill shared that since 2016 a serious schism had been growing between student groups, as evidenced by misunderstandings and a lack of trust. This challenge was rooted in the backgrounds and culture differences of minority students from southern California, minority students from southern Idaho, the majority Caucasian student population from across Idaho and what appeared at times as the often less visible LGBT population. The conflict was exasperated by the nation-wide political divisiveness that was continuing to increase. It was Dr. Gill's goal to use this initiative for the student groups to gain a greater understanding of differences and acknowledgement of their commonalities (T. Stewart, personal communication, August 19, 2019).

The day's program included three events. First, Stewart addressed the student body at 10:30 a.m. on the topic "Social Justice Requires Courage and Action: Campuses, College Students, and Grassroots Organizing." The address was divided into four sections: What is Social Justice, Personal Stories of Victims, Celebration of Diversity, and Call to Action for Justice. Second, Gissel and Stewart met in the afternoon in a private session with a cross section of BSU minority students. Third, Giseel spoke to the community at large in the evening on the topic "From Hate to Hope: How Idahoans Defeated White Nationalists—and How You Can Too." Each session also included a Q & A period (Boise State MLK Jr/Living Legacy Committee, 1910 W University Dr., Boise, ID (2020), n.d.).

The follow-up of the day's events included not only positive feedback but also video provided by the speakers that would be used by classes to encourage openness, inclusion and ways to support diversity and human rights on campus while embracing free speech.

2018 AND BEYOND: THE WORK CONTINUES

In July 2018, a youth minister and his youth group attended a religious church service in Coeur d'Alene. After the service, they were targeted by an older man as they ordered ice cream at a Coeur d'Alene fast-food restaurant. The youth minister, who was of Hispanic ancestry, was physically attacked and shoved to the ground, while the perpetrator yelled vile and racist words at the minister and the racially diverse youth. The KCTFHR worked with the Coeur d'Alene Police and Kootenai County Prosecutor on behalf of the victims. On December 20, the defendant was found guilty by a local jury of physical assault and given the maximum sentence of six months in jail by the judge.

2019 began with the KCTFHR traditions of the 34th annual Dr. Martin Luther King, Jr. Children's Program on January 15 and the 22nd annual human rights banquet on April 12. Since the inception of the kids' program, Dr. King's birthday has been celebrated with over 37,000 fifth-grade Post Falls and Coeur d'Alene students. Idaho State Senator Cherie Buckner Webb, the first African American to be elected to the Idaho State Senate, was the banquet keynote that year. Due to the banquet's generous benefactors, and in partnership with the North Idaho College Foundation, 96 minority student scholarships to have been awarded to students attending North Idaho College.

When philanthropist Gregory C. Carr purchased the former Aryan Nations compound in Hayden, Idaho he removed all indictors the neo-Nazi presence and then deeded it to the North Idaho College Foundation. In April of 2019, following a recommendation from the KCTFHR, the NIC Foundation announced the property would be sold and the proceeds would be used as seed money to establish the permanent Gregory C. Carr Visiting Professor Chair at North Idaho College.

The challenges and tensions require vigilance. In early spring 2019 local elected officials voted to support entry to the US for an Austrian who was investigated for connections to the New Zeland mass mosque shootings (Associated Press, 2019b).   In the summer of 2019, a group of Idaho state representatives sent a letter to BSU President Marlene Trump requesting that many of the cultural diversity programs at BSU be ended. Copies of the state legislators' letter were forwarded to all the other Idaho institutions of higher education as well as to the Idaho State Board of Education. The KCTFHR organized a response in support of the BSU cultural diversity programs with cosigners Bonner County Human Rights Task Force, Boundary County Human Rights Task Force, and the Coeur d'Alene based HREI. The letter to the BSU President was also forwarded to all the other Idaho institutions of higher education as well as to the Idaho State Board of Education. The July 22 letter to the BSU President in part stated "We were highly concerned and deeply troubled when we learned of the letter to your office from 28 state legislators objecting to the outstanding framework that BSU has developed and embraced to make the campus a safe, accepting, friendly and inclusive environment. To do otherwise, would result in a major setback for a campus that cherishes social justice for all its students, employees and visitors" (T. Stewart, personal communication, August, 19, 2019).

During the July 4th Coeur d'Alene Chamber of Commerce Parade, an excavation and landscaping company created a parade entry that displayed the confederate flag plus a sign of a young African American child eating a piece of watermelon with pickaninny imagery from the 1920s. Evidence of the community's outrage was found in the Sunday, July 28 edition of the "Coeur d'Alene Press," which ran a lead story covering the reactions of the community regarding the incident. On behalf of parade sponsor, the Coeur d'Alene Chamber of Commerce CEO Steve Wilson stated: "Unfortunately one parade entry exhibited graphic displays that are totally inconsistent with the values of the Chamber or the celebratory intent of our parade."

On behalf of the KCTFHR, Stewart stated in part: "When you find that type of message you have to call it what it is. It's racism . . . any time you demean another race or minority or community, any time you degrade them, it meets the definition of racism." KCTFHR President Christie Wood and Stewart later met with Steve Wilson, the Chamber CEO, and came up with new guidelines and principles for all future Chamber parades.

The work of the KCTFHR has demonstrated a broad range of nonviolent strategies. Stewart, who would claim to be an ordinary person, along with many other members of the Inland Northwest have done extraordinary things to stand up to hate. According to Stewart, for those inspired to work for the advancement of social justice, he would share this advice from the late Dr. Martin Luther King, Jr.: "There comes a time when one must take a position that is neither safe nor politic nor popular, but he must take it because his conscience tells him it is right."

DISCUSSION QUESTIONS

1.

Briefly describe the situation in the case. What aspects of your description are judgments (value statements about what is good or bad) and what aspects are objective statements?

2.

What was the significance of the Kennans v. Aryan Nation civil trial? What strategies were used in this instance to overcome hate? How can they be useful today?

3.

In the other examples highlighted in this case study, what were other strategies the KCTFHR used to overcome hate? Could these strategies still be applicable today?

4.

What goal(s) can you envision for the outcomes in this case? Brainstorm new strategies for reaching the goal(s). What are the strengths and limitations of each?

5.

What lessons do you take away from this case and how might you apply them in your own context?

REFERENCES

ABC News. (2006, January 7). *Aryan nations gives up compound*. Retrieved March 3, 2020, from ABC News. https://abcnews.go.com/US/story?id=95672&page=1

About Human Rights Education Institute. (n.d.). Retrieved March 3, 2020, from http://hrei.org/about/

Associated Press. (2019a, April 18). *Foundation to sell former site of Aryan Nations compound*. Retrieved March 3, 2020, from Federal News Network. https://federalnewsnetwork.com/government-news/2019/04/foundation-to-sell-former-site-of-aryan-nations-compound/

Associated Press. (2019b, May 25). *Hate makes a comeback in the Pacific Northwest*. Retrieved March 3, 2020, from *Los Angeles Times*. https://www.latimes.com/nation/nationnow/la-fg-pacific-northwest-hate-20190525-story.html

Balch, W. R. (2006). The rise and fall of Aryan nations. A resource mobilization perspective. *Journal of Political and Military Sociology, 34*(1), 81–113. Retrieved from https://login.proxy.foley.gonzaga.edu/login?url=https://search.proquest.com/docview/206653566?accountid=1557

Bindel, J. (2014, October 26). *The truth behind America's most famous gay-hate murder*. Retrieved from the Guardian. https://www.theguardian.com/world/2014/oct/26/the-truth-behind-americas-most-famous-gay-hate-murder-matthew-shepard

Boise State MLK Jr/Living Legacy Committee, 1910 W University Dr., Boise, ID (2020). (n.d.). Retrieved March 3, 2020, from www.findglocal.com. http://www.findglocal.com/US/Boise/149120431806863/Boise-State-MLK-Jr-Living-Legacy-Committee

Boise State News. (2017, September 27). Marilyn Shuler human rights initiative to host advocates, leaders Oct. 26. *Boise State News*. Retrieved April 16, 2020, from Boise State News. https://www.boisestate.edu/news/2017/09/27/marilyn-shuler-human-rights-initiative-to-host-advocates-leaders-oct-26/

Cockle, R., & Oregonian, T. (2012, August 28). *20 years after Ruby Ridge siege, extremists are fewer in northern Idaho but still remain*. Retrieved March 3, 2020, from oregonlive. https://www.oregonlive.com/pacific-northwest-news/2012/08/20_years_after_ruby_ridge_sieg.html

Deshais, N. (2019, March 14). *Southern Poverty Law Center fires co-founder Morris Dees, civil rights attorney behind bankruptcy of North Idaho's Aryan Nations*. Retrieved March 3, 2020, from AP NEWS. https://apnews.com/4159490cef4049539aae9f012f171147

Graman, K. (2010, October 22). Kansas hate group met by strong opposition at each stop. *The Spokesman-Review*. Retrieved March 3, 2020, from www.spokesman.com. https://www.spokesman.com/stories/2010/oct/22/dueling-demonstrations/

Guilhem, M. (2017, October 2). *Legacy of hate: Human rights task force talks Aryan Nations and North Idaho culture*. Retrieved March 3, 2020, from www.boisestatepublicradio.org. https://www.boisestatepublicradio.org/post/legacy-hate-human-rights-task-force-talks-aryan-nations-and-north-idaho-culture#stream/0

Healey, J. (2017, Spetember 21). Love Lives Here. The Reader. https://sandpointreader.com/love-lives-here/

Hult, K. (2011 September, n.d.). *Fig tree—kootenai county task force 30 years*. Retrieved from www.thefigtree.org. http://www.thefigtree.org/sept11/090711KootenaiTFHR.html

Hult, K. (2016). *Monthly newspaper and website covering faith in action throughout the Inland Northwest online at www.thefigtree.org · check The Fig Tree Facebook page daily for news and links, 33*, 535–1813. Retrieved from https://www.thefigtree.org/may16/May16FT.pdf

KCTFHR. (n.d.a). *About*. https://www.idahohumanrights.org/about.html

KCTFHR. (n.d.b). *History*. www.idahohumanrights.org, https://www.idahohumanrights.org/history.html

KHQ. (2009, August 21). *"We will not be known as communities who tolerate hate," says Spokane mayor*. https://www.khq.com/news/we-will-not-be-known-as-communities-who-tolerate-hate/article_82f4e441-63c1-595e-9afc-fc06a209708f.html

Morlin, B. (2012, November 11). Neo-Nazi builds North Idaho compound to replace defunct Aryan Nations. Southern Poverty Law Center. https://www.splcenter.org/fighting-hate/intelligence-report/2012/neo-nazi-builds-north-idaho-compound-replace-defunct-aryan-nations

Morlin, B. (2017, September 7). CenterHate Literature in E-mail Flyers Hits Sandpoint, Idaho. Southern Poverty Law Center. https://www.splcenter.org/hatewatch/2017/09/07/hate-literature-e-mail-flyers-hits-sandpoint-idaho

North Idaho College Sentinel, The Vol. 68 No. 6 February 9, 2015. (n.d.). Retrieved March 3, 2020, from Issuu. https://issuu.com/molsteadlibraryatnic/docs/nic_sentinel_spring_2015__issue__1

NW Coalition for Human Rights—Working for social justice and equality in the Pacific Northwest. (n.d.). Retrieved March 3, 2020, from http://www.nwcoalitionhumanrights.org/

Racist flyers distributed in Spokane Valley. (n.d.). Retrieved April 16, 2020, from KHQ Right Now. https://www.khq.com/news/racist-flyers-distributed-in-spokane-valley/article_e6941dcc-081c-585d-bbb9-de26a29c708d.html

Southern Law Poverty Law Center, Keenan v. Aryan Nations. (n.d.). Retrieved March 3, 2020, from Southern Poverty Law Center. https://www.splcenter.org/seeking-justice/case-docket/keenan-v-aryan-nations

Spokesman Review, The (2012, November 27). Racist Building New Aryan Compound. https://www.spokesman.com/blogs/hbo/2012/nov/27/racist-building-new-aryan-compound/

Stewart, T., & Gissel, N. (2012). Choosing social justice over hate: Two stories of community success in the Pacific Northwest. *National Civic Review, 101*(2), 38–43. Retrieved from https://doi.org/10.1002/ncr.21075

Chapter 4

THE STORY IN TENNESSEE

© Olinchuk/Shutterstock.com

OVERVIEW

Pulaski, Tennessee is a small town with a population of less than 8,000 people (U.S. Census Bureau, 2018). The community is home to the Tennessee College of Applied Technology-Pulaski (TCAT) and to Martin Methodist College. It is also the birth place of what we now know as the *Ku Klux Klan (KKK)* (Lewis & Serbu, 1999). The story of the rise of the Klan, its short-lived existence, its rebirth in the 1920s and again in 1980s is also a demonstration of the resiliency of the citizens of Pulaski to rise up and define their community, not as a place that embraces racism, but instead as a community "striving to develop new traditions and a welcoming environment for all residents and visitors" (City of Pulaski, 1809, p. 1). How did this small-town community become the target for highly visible racist activity, getting thrust into the national spotlight? Why was Pulaski chosen to be the site of annual Klan "homecoming marches" (Blee, 2003, p. 170)? What can we learn from Pulaski's struggles and strategies that is useful in our own communities?

Timeline

1865	First Klan Meeting
1867	Passage of the Tennessee KKK Act
1868	Pulaski Race Riots
1869	Murder of Capt. Seymour Barmore, Resignation of Tennessee Gov. Brownlow Disbanding of the Klan
1915	D.W. Grifith's Birth of a Nation and the Rebirth of the Knights of the KKK
1917	Pulaski KKK Commemorative Plaque Celebration
1986	First observance of Dr. MLK Jr. Day and First Pulaski Klan Homecoming March
1989	Formation of Nonprofit Giles Countians United, Aryan Nations March at Klan Homecoming, and Passage of Pulaski Ordinance No. 14
1990	Pulaski Recognized by National Civic League Award and Sen. Al Gore
2017	Social Media Campaign "Ban the KKK Rally in Pulaski, TN" (Sign the Petition, 2017. p. 1)
2019	Tennessee Governor Declares July 13 as Nathan Bedford Forrest Day.

Allison, 2019; History.com Editors, 2018; Newton, 2014; Newton & Newton, 1991; Sign the Petition, 2017

TAKE NOTICE

The Ku Klux Klan will assemble at their usual place of rendezvous, 'The Den,' on Tuesday night next, exactly at the hour of midnight, in costume and bearing the arms of the Klan. By order of the Grand Cyclops.

(Pulaski Citizen, 1867, as cited in Sims, 1996).

1865 TO 1869: RECONSTRUCTION AND UPHOLDING THE LAW (PULASKI, TENNESSEE; UNDOING OF THE RECONSTRUCTION ERA "KKK")

In December of 1865, six young veterans of the Confederate Army founded the KKK—John Lester, John Kennedy, James Crowe, Frank McCord, Richard Reed, and Calvin Jones (Lewis & Serbu, 1999. Sitting in the Pulaski law offices of Judge Thomas Jones, father of Calvin Jones, the young men decided to form a social club, calling themselves "kuklos," from the Greek word meaning "circle" or "band." (Bartoletti, 2010, p. 25). The group was concerned about losing power and privilege due to Reconstruction after the Civil War and what they considered the occupation of the South by Federal troops (Library of Congress, 1870). The Klan formed a statewide organization in April of 1867 at a meeting in the Maxwell Hotel in Nashville. Nathan Bedford Forrest of Memphis became the "Grand Wizard" at this 1867 gathering (Carney, 2001). He was both a former confederate general (considered by some to be a hero) and slave trader. Women could not officially join the initial Klan, although they played significant roles by sewing uniforms and generally supporting their husbands, sons, and brothers who were members (Pinar, 2001). The "need" to protect White women as damsels in distress motivated violence, as supported by "Grand Wizard" Forrest when he said "Ladies were ravished by some of those negroes" (Langguth, 2015, p. 290) and the Klan could deal with the problem better than the law.

Grand Wizard Forrest flexed his muscle by going after Tennessee Gov. Parson Brownlow. Gov. Brownlow was an abolitionist. He opposed secession and he supported reconstruction (Coulter, 1999, p. 136). The Klan's extreme violence prompted government officials, including Brownlow, to pass the KKK Act in 1867 in which Klan members were fined and faced five years in jail (Alexander, 1949). The Klan was responsible for multiple acts of terror, assault, and killing that lead President Ulysses S. Grant to sign the act into federal law in 1871 that effectively outlawed the Klan (Conklin, n.d.).

This was also the era when tensions in the community erupted resulting in the 1868 Pulaski race riot and a terrible blight in the history of the community (Robinson, 2017). More than a dozen White men shot at Black men in a Black-owned grocery store. It was reported that while none of the White people were injured or prosecuted, one Black man was murdered, one mortally wounded, and an additional four Black men were injured (Riot Against Negros in Pulaski, Tennessee, 1868, 1868).

POINTS TO PONDER

Are the statements in this paragraph more objective or judgmental? An objective statement is made with as little bias as humanly possible. A judgmental statement involves an evaluation from a particular standpoint of something's worth, being good or bad, better or worse, right or wrong. Saying the 1886 Pulaski race riots were "a terrible blight" is an evaluative statement judging the event as bad or wrong. Reporting the facts that "none of the White people were injured or prosecuted, one Black man was murdered, one mortally wounded, and an additional four Black men were injured" is an objective statement. Think of an example of when you had disagreed with someone. Was the disagreement over an objective statement or a judgmental statement? How do you handle disagreement if it is based on objective statement(s)? On judgments?

Gov. Brownlow hired Capt. Seymour Barmore of Cincinnati to infiltrate the Klan. Capt. Barmore dressed in a Klan costume, traveled to Pulaski, began to attend meetings, and gathered names of Klan members (Bartoletti, 2010). When Brownlow was traveling by train to Nashville, he left a notebook in his boarding room that was found by Klan members. Capt. Barmore's train was stopped in Columbia and his body was recovered in February 1869 from the Duck River. He had a rope around his neck and a bullet in his skull, apparently killed for infiltrating the Klan (Edward, 2013).

On February 25th, 1869, Brownlow resigned as Governor and his successor began eliminating or reversing reconstruction legislation (Edward, 2013). Once Gov. Brownlow was out of office, "Grand Wizard" Forrest decided that Klan masks and costumes should be destroyed and ordered the disbanding of the Klan (Newton, 2014, p. 16). According to some, the order was issued as a means to stop excessive violence while others suggest that the formal KKK organization was no longer necessary due to political opposition no longer being in office.

1915 TO 1944: CRIMINAL JUSTICE RESPONDS TO MURDER AND VIOLENCE (PULASKI, TENNESSEE: COUNTERING BIRTH OF A NATION AND KKK COMMEMORATION)

D.W. Griffith's "Birth Of A Nation" (Griffith, Dixon, & Triangle Film Corporation, 1915) was a major motion picture that depicted the loss of the South during the Civil War. The film gained some of its notoriety because it was screened in the White House for Woodrow Wilson. Inspired in part by the images created by D.W. Griffith, a new Klan was born in 1915 outside of Atlanta, Georgia. A man by the name of William J. Simmons proclaimed the rebirth of the Knights of the KKK by lighting a wooden cross on fire (Pinar, 2001). The advertisement taken out in the Atlanta newspaper read: "The World's Greatest Secret, Social, Patriotic, Fraternal, Beneficiary Order" and a "High Class Order for Men of Intelligence and Character" (Rothman, 2016, p. 2).

Pulaski was not to be forgotten when it came to the birth of the original Klan. In 1917, the local women's Chapter of the United Daughters of the

Image of Stonewall, Georgia monument

Confederacy organized the unveiling of a bronze commemorative plaque to mark the founding of the Klan (Newbill, 1917, p. 355).

The plaque names the initial founders of the Klan and reads "KKK organized in this, the law office of Judge Thomas M. Jones, Dec. 24, 1865" (Jackson, 1973, p. 65). The event was well attended while a local pastor exclaimed that the Klan was an "army of defense and a safeguard of virtue" (Willson, 1980, p. 113). During one address at the gathering, Mr. Mc Cord, proposed that the town rechristen old Madison Street as "Ku Klux Avenue" (Newbill, 1917, p. 355) and the crowd overwhelmingly approved by a show of hands. "In honoring these men, we express but faintly the grateful recognition which is due them from all the people of our beloved southland" said Mrs. Grace Meredith Newbill, President, Giles County Chapter U.D.C. July, 1917 (Newbill, 1917, p. 355).

POINTS TO PONDER

From the perspective of the Chapter of the United Daughters of the Confederacy, placing a commemorative plaque on the building where the first Klan meeting was held in Pulaski was a good strategy because it honored their values for security, safety, societal stability, and relationships. From your own value system, are there actions you have taken that honor your values for security, safety, societal stability, and relationships (e.g., work hard to maintain employment, celebrate family traditions, etc.)?

© Everett Historical/Shutterstock.com

Images of the KKK marches in Washington, DC, circa 1920

It was this 1920s Klan that made bigotry, intimidation, harassment, and violence defensible in the name of patriotism by stable middle-class White protestant families (Rothman, 2016). This incarnation of the Klan grew into a national movement, attracting educated and powerful people in society (elected officials, professionals, and police officers, alike). Approximately five hundred thousand women made up the newly formed WKKK, the Women of the KKK, who were empowered after the suffrage movement to be a part of civic life. These women lobbied for national quotas for immigration, racial segregation, and promoted the "eternal supremacy" of the White race in opposition to the "rising tide of color" (Smith, 2018, p. 1). Men and women Klan members were concerned with immigration reform based on anti-Eastern European, anti-Catholic, and Anti-Semitic views. They framed their arguments around moral reform and their membership grew to more than four million members by some counts. Of note, the KKK marched with more than 50,000 members down Pennsylvania Avenue in Washington, D.C. in 1925. Many wore robes of various colors with a red circular patch and a cross with a drop of blood at its center. Many politicians, particularly in states including Indiana and Oregon, were publicly endorsed by the Klan and it was not uncommon for elected officials to be active Klan members. Although cities such as Philadelphia and Pittsburgh may have supported a statewide human rights commission, outlying Pennsylvania communities were more open to Klan participation.

The states with the largest enrollments between 1915 and 1944 were Indiana, Ohio, Texas, and Pennsylvania (Rothman, 2016). Membership in the Klan declined before participation increased again after the *Brown v. Board of Education* Supreme Court decision in 1954 and the passage of the 1964 Civil Rights Act (Civil Rights Era, 1950–1963—The Civil Rights Act of 1964: A long struggle for freedom, Exhibitions—Library of Congress, 2010). Members of the Klan continued to be found guilty of tremendous acts of terror, including the assassination of Medgar Evers; the 1963 bombing that killed four Black girls Cynthia Wesley, Carole Robertson, Addie Mae Collins, and Denise McNair in a Birmingham church; the 1964 murders of three civil rights workers James Chaney, Andrew Goodman, and Michael Schwerner; the 1966 death of a civil rights leader Vernon Ferdinand Dahmer; and the 1981 murder of Michael Donald, a Black man whose beaten, slashed body was hanged from a tree (White, 2000).

1980S: INSPIRED BY REV. KELLY AND THE CREATION OF GILES COUNTY UNITED (PULASKI, TENNESSEE: COUNTERING THE KLAN HOMECOMING)

© BestStockFoto/Shutterstock.com

Map to locate Pulaski, Tennessee

Today, Pulaski, Tennessee is a town of less than 8,000 residents located approximately 90 miles south of Nashville and it remains the county seat of Giles County. The population of Pulaski has grown from 1,134 in 1850, to 2,928 in 1910, 5,314 in 1940, and 7,184 in 1980 (U.S. Census Bureau, 2018). Like many U.S. communities during the late 19th and early 20th centuries, Pulaski had segregated bathrooms and drinking. Community member Dan Speer said "Growing up during that period, you know, it was just—it just didn't seem right to me that people were treated that way, you know. Separate—in their own school—and things. And I knew, even as a kid, I knew they didn't get the resources they needed to have" (Alford, n.d.).

In the 1980s, many of the town's adults had grown up in a segregated culture, but took pride in playing together as children of different races and Pulaski was the first community in the state of Tennessee to voluntarily integrate schools (Alford, n.d.).

POINTS TO PONDER

Why did the practice of children of different races playing together and integrated schools support Dan Speer's sense that segregation was bad ("it just didn't seem right")? What symbols, language, celebrations, stories, practices, and so on are a part of your lived experience and inform what is important in your family? Place of work? Neighborhood?

© mark reinstein/Shutterstock.com

1983, President Ronald Reagan signing the law recognizing Dr. Martin Luther King, Jr. Day

Thom Robb was not from Tennessee, but he had met David Duke and Robb had been active in the White resistance movement. After he joined the Klan, Robb wanted to become the Klan's National Director. Although Dr. Martin Luther King (MLK) Jr. was assassinated in 1968, it wasn't until 1983 that President Ronald Reagan signed the law recognizing Dr. MLK Jr. Day as a federal holiday and the first MLK Jr. observance was planned for January 1986 (Travers, 2006). It was during 1985 that Robb came up with the idea to hold a protest on that first MLK national holiday in Pulaski, the birthplace of the Klan (Newton, 2014, p. 202). Grand Wizard Stanley McCollum of Alabama applied for the parade permit and City Attorney Jack Henry said the Klan had a right to march as long as members wore no hoods and did not litter or obstruct traffic (A Brief History of the Ku Klux Klan, 1996). The weather in Pulaski in January, 1986 was mild and a small number of people participated near the town square where the first Klan meeting had taken place in 1865. Marchers gathered at the courthouse to hear the speech of the Grand Wizard (Alford, n.d.).

The "Klan Homecoming" marches were first held on January 18, 1986, January 17, 1987, January 16, 1988, and January 14, 1989. They gained attention from local and national media, which stirred up a racist reputation for Pulaski. Media interviewed members of the Pulaski community, asking how they felt about the marches. As one storeowner put it, "Please look at the license tags around the square. They're not Giles County. They are from Pennsylvania, they're from Ohio, they're from Alabama, they're from Texas, you know, these are not local people that are coming to the marches." A group of Pulaski citizens lead in part by the local Rev. Gary Kelly, set out to make a statement of their own.

The Pulaski community was frustrated with the marches and those feelings were mounting to crisis levels and feeling threatened. The community wanted to define itself as a tourist destination and the Klan marches and reputation for condoning hatred didn't match their goals. Some community members wanted to ignore the marches, hoping the Klan would fade away. Garry Kelly, minister of the local First Presbyterian Church, voiced opposition to the Klan and their marches starting with the first march in 1986. The minister had just completed the seminary and was in his mid-20s. He held a protest sign at the town square during the march that read: "Red and yellow, black and white, we're all precious in God's sight" (Alford, n.d.). The Klan marchers were not so quiet according to Rev. Kelly, who heard them call him names including "N____ lover" and "commie queer." Men, women, and children would form the up-raised arm salute, shouting, "White Power!" "Hang a n_____!" "Burn a Jew!" In each of the following years when the marchers came to Pulaski, Rev. Kelly would go to his attic, looking for his "Klan sign" and protest all over again.

POINTS TO PONDER

Rev. Kelly was an inspirational leader to members of the Pulaski community, not only because of his title as a minister, but also because of the actions he took. His quiet, inexpensive, and informal, sign reading "Red and yellow, black and white, we're all precious in God's sight" influenced others through the simple act of modeling leadership. In what ways have you been inspired by someone, not because they had a job title, but because you chose to listen and learn from their actions? Why do you consider that person a leader?

The simple act of Rev. Kelly protesting with his handmade sign that first year of the Klan march in Pulaski and each year thereafter inspired other community members. A group of them gathered and asked the media not to cover the march as a news story. To counter the media's needs for covering public interest stories, the community began brainstorming options that would give the media something else to report on besides Pulaski as home of the Klan. They became educated about the Klan, created a speaker's bureau to talk about the Klan and why opposition was important. They successfully lobbied for the passage of state hate crime laws. The group arranged poster contests; petition drives were started. According to Bob Henry "we got a lot of people on board, despite a lot of early opposition, a lot of early opposition from elected officials, and other people" (Alford, n.d.). The opposition's concern was that the community should be ignoring the Klan and not giving the Klan additional attention and publicity.

In 1989, Bettie Higgins was the Executive Director of the Chamber of Commerce and she met with the Pulaski mayor. "Oh, we just ignore them. They leave right afterwards" (Alford, n.d.). The mayor told Bettie when she asked what could be done about the Klan marches. She had overheard that a second group applied for a parade permit and learned that "The Aryan Nations of the Church of Jesus Christ, Identity" from Coeur d' Alene (CDA), Idaho, would be joining the Klan march in Pulaski that year (Alford, n.d.). The Aryan Nations had decided that Pulaski would make a better headquarters than CDA. The parade would be a place for them to demonstrate their strength and build a home base. The group had purchased land, raised flags, and were ready to move.

Bob Henry took it upon himself to create a nonprofit Giles Countians United and was elected the first president of it. Bettie Higgins recruited members including Rev. Kelly and others that provided a diverse coalition—Black, White, male, female, Methodist, Baptist, Episcopal, Catholic, Presbyterian. The group met weekly, as a grassroots movement.

Bettie Higgins contacted the chamber of commerce in CDA, Idaho, which was the home of the Aryan Nations. The CDA Chamber referred Ms. Higgins to Tony Stewart of the Kootenai County Task Force on Human Relations (KCTFHR) because the group had years of experience supporting victims and organizing against the Aryan Nations. Through multiple consultations during the month of July 1989, Stewart proposed three coordinated strategies to Bettie and her group added other ideas such as renting all the motel rooms. Together, these would need to be implemented simultaneously to "boycott" the Aryan Nations. First, any and all community members could display orange ribbons to create a sense of empowerment and self-determination. Second, stores placed signs in their windows explicitly stating that they supported human rights. And third, when the Aryan Nations came to march, the community created a ghost town—there were few (nonlaw enforcement) people in attendance and the march had no audience. Even all of the Pulaski businesses agreed to close their stores and join the residents out of town.

Reflecting on the Klan's TV message of how the Klan brought money into the local economy, the Giles Countians United reframed their own message

". . . we don't want their money" (Alford, n.d.). The United members visited town retailers, inviting the owners to close their shops on Saturday (the most popular shopping day), specifically the Saturday of the Klan march. More and more shop owners agreed to close their stores, including the local McDonalds. When the headquarters for Wal-Mart in Bentonville, Arkansas realized their restrooms would likely be the only ones open, their legal department decided Wal-Mart would close too. Shops closed throughout the whole county. For the motels and hotels that would not close, the United group purchased all of the rooms. The local Retail Merchants Association had posters printed—"This Store Will Be Closed When the Aryan Nation Comes to Town—we are closing in support of Brotherhood" (Alford, n.d.). Each week the Untied group used a part of the newspaper page to print a "Scroll of Honor" of local merchants who had agreed to close, recognizing that closing their shops was a serious statement of putting their money where their mouth was. To carry out the three KCTFHR strategies, people in Pulaski started placing orange ribbons on antennas of cars, store owners put ribbons on their front doors and trees; every police vehicle had orange ribbons. Orange ribbons could be found on nearly every building, home, and even on people's sleeves and in children's hair. As florists ran out of orange ribbon, people got orange highway tape from the transportation department. Some people created orange ribbon wreaths and one was even hung around the neck of the Confederate soldier's statue in the center of town along the parade route. The event got media coverage from a Nashville TV station and people sent letters of support to the Pulaski community. Ministers brought youth groups to Pulaski for multi-ethnic prayer services where people prayed together. Pulaski community member Wendy Hibdon noted the day of the march was a very proud moment in her life, saying about the Klan marches "This is not us. We don't agree to this. We are not prejudiced. And we believe in brotherhood" (Alford, n.d.).

When the Klan came to town to march that year, they didn't have a place to go to the bathroom, to eat, sleep, or shop. The Klan couldn't buy gas, medicine, or get a meal. The goal was to do something peaceful that would make a statement that the community was turning their backs on the extremists. The community couldn't stop the Aryan Nations from coming to

Pulaski, it was their right to come. Although Pulaski had the right to not be gracious hosts, when the marchers applied for a parade permit, they were treated like human beings, the same way all parade applicants were treated. According to Pulaski police officer John White, "I treated them like they was human beings, like I'd want to be treated" (Alford, n.d.).

Stanley Newton was Chief of Police and he considered his job was to keep the peace—which included discouraging visitors and citizens alike to stay away from town on the day of the march. One of the best sources for background on Klan activities at that time was the Jewish Anti-defamation League and they could inform the community of who was planning on attending marches from various states. The day of the march, every available Tennessee Department of Corrections bus was loaded with razor wire on the windows and parked one-half block off the square to be used as overflow for the jail, if needed. The Tennessee Highway Patrol drove every police car that they could find and parked them right next to the buses. The Patrol members took out their shields, and started beating their shields as they walked up the street. Other off-duty officers from Fayetteville, Lincoln County, Marshall County, Wayne County, Lawrence County, and possibly Alabama joined in the show of police force. Armed plainclothes officers lined the square. Emergency medical treatment centers were set up and a police helicopter circled overhead.

POINTS TO PONDER

Officers John White and Stanley Newton are White. What impact would knowing the race/color of all of the stakeholders make in your understanding of the case? What race/color did you imagine each person in the case is and why?

The 1989 Klan march in Pulaski happened without incident. No one was arrested. There was no property damage. No one was hurt. And over the next 20 years, the Aryan Nations did not return to be a part of the march again. And Aryan Nations leader Richard Butler never returned to Pulaski before his death in 2004.

There were significant risks for harm and violence and none of that came to be in this case. The Boycott as it later came to be known did have its detractors. Many of the Giles Countians United members had been threatened and some were sued. Tires were slashed, stores lost money by closing on the day of the march. Notices were left on doors: "The Knights of the KKK is watching you, and we don't like what we see" (Human Rights Watch, 1996). Pulaski organizers were instructed to use precautions opening mail. People were trained to not take the same route home every day and to consider leaving town during certain periods when the Klan came to town. An organizer was even shot at. Some people wanted the 1917 KKK commemorative plaque removed. Others wanted it to remain as a significant historical marker. The owners of the building where the KKK founding plaque was located had the plaque turned backward so that the inscription was hidden, and reattached in the same place on the building as a literal statement of turning away from the Klan.

In late 1989, both the Klan and Giles Countians United were preparing for January 13, 1990, the MLK holiday. The city had passed Ordinance No. 14 1989 that allowed for only one parade on any given day with the purposes of mitigating costs and expenses to the city. All others applying for a permit for the same date would be denied. The City would "only grant one parade permit per month; that permits would be granted to the first applicant for a given date; that permit applications were required to be filed no sooner than 180 days and no later than 45 days prior to the proposed parade date; that permits would not be granted if a conflicting event had already been scheduled; that permits would not be granted if the City anticipated violence; that permits would not be granted to groups that advocated unlawful acts, racial intimidation, or the overthrow of the government; that permits would not be granted for parades of more than 250 marchers; and that marchers were not allowed to wear masks or disguises"(M.D. Tennessee, 1990).

With this new ordinance, the Giles Countian United group made sure to submit a parade permit first for the date of the MLK holiday. Thom Robb applied for a "Klan Homecoming" permit after the United application, and when the Klan permit was rejected, Robb claimed KKK's parade permit was "lawfully secured by the fact that such rallies which have traditionally been held on the Saturday before MLK's National Holiday are now a long-standing custom" (M.D. Tennessee, 1990).

In January 13, 1990, the Klan showed up to march on the edge of town, although they did not have a permit. Instead of a march, they called it a press conference with several hundred people in attendance. Thom Robb was cited by the police and given a court date for later in January. The Giles Countian United Brotherhood march had been approved to march that day. There was discussion about calling the Brotherhood parade off due to concerns that the Klan wanted to break up the march and there could be violence. However, the United Brotherhood march did take place as a sign of solidarity for the community, with crowds cheering and applauding along the sidewalk. Marchers dressed in orange and white walked in the parade behind the banner, "The Spirit of Pulaski." United Brotherhood events were held every year for several years thereafter and created a sense of genuine community empowerment.

A 1990 ABC news broadcast named Pulaski its "Person of The Week." Responding to the work of Giles Countians United's successful efforts to counter the KKK, U.S. Senator Al Gore (D), TN wrote: "your courageous demonstration of unity and brotherhood in the face of the Aryan Nations hate-filled profession of bigotry and division is commendable. Their march in Pulaski was another attempt to garner publicity. But it failed. It failed because of you. You turned the tables on the Aryan Nations. I am proud of your efforts and your example to our country. Sincerely, Al Gore, United States Senator." (Pulaski, 1990).

21st Century: The work continues	1990	2000	2010	2017
Total population	7,895	7,871	7,870	7,643
White	73%	70%	71%	69%
Black or African American	27%	27%	24%	24%
Two or more races or other	0%	3%	5%	7%

U.S. Census Bureau, (2018).

Marches continue; strategies to counter hate continue; divisiveness and unrest continues. At the 1992 Pulaski Klan Homecoming march, Confederate flags, Nazi battle flags, and hand-painted signs saying "God Hates N**gers," "Join The KKK," and "Save the White Race. Unite!" (Picciolini, 2018), were visible. The Klan convened the 11th annual Nathan Bedford Forrest birthday march in July 2009. In 2014, the city of Pulaski organized a multi-pronged effort to reframe and remember their history as a celebration of local heroes, depicting their stories and images through art. In an interview in 2015, Thom Robb and his daughter, Rachel Pendergraft, explained their position with the Klan and European Heritage Festivals this way: "I don't hate black people. We're not against people of color, I don't hate them, they can't help they were born black. So I don't hate them for that. But I am concerned about the future of our people. What kind of future they're gonna have? Uh, we do feel that white people are facing genocide. And so we preach, I guess you could say, what we call a message of White Christian Revival. Our nation, as far as we're concerned, is living in open rebellion against God. And that's in the areas of this recent [Supreme Court] ruling of sodomy, but also in the areas of race. We feel that racially we are living in open rebellion to God also. And so our message is that people need to repent of the rebellion against God . . . What we're really about is taking a message of hope and deliverance to our people" (KKK group wants to preserve "our own slice of heaven," 2015).

In 2017, the Giles Countians United created a "Ban the KKK Rally in Pulaski Tennessee" petition on www.Change.org, getting 984 supporters (Sign the Petition, 2017). That same year, in a media interview about how to address the Klan march, a member of the Pulaski City Council said: "Turning our back on it was the most effective way to deal with it. Because of that, although they do still come back once a year, barely anyone comes. Our businesses are still open, and we just basically ignore what they're doing" (Caloway, 2017). She went on to say "Those groups, I feel, want publicity, exposure, validation, and the way that Pulaski has chosen to deal with their visits has not given them any of those things that they covet, in my opinion" (Caloway, 2017). The impact of the community strategies to counter hate can in part be measured by the story of Christian Piccolini, a White supremacist who marched in the Pulaski "Klan Homecoming" parades and later left a violent neo-Nazi skinhead group in which he had played a significant leadership role.

True transformational change is complicated. One regular at a Pulaski bar, who was also a member of the Klan felt that the Klan was misunderstood. "What always bothers me, is people think we're racist. It bothers me. I don't know what we do to make people think we're racist" (Alford, n.d.). And then Gov. Bill Lee signed a proclamation in 2019 declaring Saturday, July 13, as Tennessee's Nathan Bedford Forrest Day (Allison, 2019).

DISCUSSION QUESTIONS

1.

Briefly describe the situation in the case. What aspects of your description are judgments (value statements about what is good or bad) and what aspects are objective statements?

2.

Officers John White and Stanley Newton described their approach to engagement with the Klan as an opportunity to connect on a human level, "I treated them like they was human beings, like I'd want to be treated." Is a dialogic approach an opportunity only afforded to someone of Caucasian descent? Would there have been a different dynamic if the officers were people of color?

3.

List multiple stakeholders in the case and identify the actions/strategies that each took. Why did each stakeholder (1965 Klan, 1920s Klan, 1980s Klan, Pulaski residents, Pulaski business owners, Media, etc.) choose a particular strategy and what criteria did they use to determine what actions would be the "right" actions to take?

4.

What symbols, language, celebrations, stories, practices, and so on are used by each stakeholder to communicate what their group thinks is important and guides the behaviors of the group?

5.

Who were the key leaders? Describe their roles and how they influenced other people to support their strategies. Was Nathan Bedford Forrest, a confederate general, a slave trader, and the first Ku Klux Klan (KKK) "Grand Wizard," a leader or not? Why or why not? What more do you want to know about Tennessee Gov. Brownlow and his resignation? What would you have done if you were in his place?

6.

What goal(s) can you envision for the outcomes in this case? Brainstorm new strategies for reaching the goal(s). What are the strengths and limitations of each?

7.

What lessons do you take away from this case and how might you apply them in your own context?

REFERENCES

A Brief History of the Ku Klux Klan. (1996). *The Journal of Blacks in Higher Education, 14*, 32. https://doi.org/10.2307/2962813

Alexander, T. B. (1949). Kukluxism in Tennessee, 1865–1869. *Tennessee Historical Quarterly, 8*(3), 195–219. https://www.jstor.org/stable/42621013

Alford, D. (n.d.). Boycott: Pulaski, Tennessee and the Legacy of the Ku Klux Klan.

Allison, N. (2019, July 12.). *Gov. Bill Lee signs Nathan Bedford Forrest Day proclamation, is not considering law change.* Retrieved February 23, 2020, from The Tennessean. https://www.tennessean.com/story/news/politics/2019/07/12/tennessee-nathan-bedford-forrest-day-gov-bill-lee-signs-proclamation/1684059001/

Bartoletti, C. S. (2010). *They called themselves the K.K.K.: The birth of an American terrorist group.* Boston, MA: Houghton Mifflin Harcourt.

Blee, K. M. (2003). *Inside organized racism: Women in the hate movement.* Berkeley, CA: University Of California Press.

Caloway, N. (2017, October 26). *Pulaski residents' advice for racially charged protests: Ignore them.* Retrieved February 17, 2020, from WKRN News 2. https://www.wkrn.com/news/pulaski-residents-advice-for-racially-charged-protests-ignore-them/

Carney, C. (2001). The contested image of Nathan Bedford Forrest. *The Journal of Southern History, 67*(3), 601. https://doi.org/10.2307/3070019

City of Pulaski. (1809). *Pulaskitennenesse.* Retrieved February 17, 2020, from www.pulaski-tn.com, http://www.pulaski-tn.com

Civil Rights Era (1950–1963)—The Civil Rights Act of 1964: A long struggle for freedom, Exhibitions—Library of Congress. (2010). Retrieved from Loc.gov. https://www.loc.gov/exhibits/civil-rights-act/civil-rights-era.html

Conklin, F. (n.d.). *William Gannaway "Parson" Brownlow.* Retrieved February 17, 2020, from Tennessee Encyclopedia. Retrieved from https://tennesseeencyclopedia.net/entries/william-gannaway-brownlow/

Coulter, M. E. (1999). *William G. Brownlow?: Fighting parson of the Southern Highlands.* Knoxville, TN. University of Tennessee Press.

Edward, W. H. (2013). *Fare well to all radicals: Redeeming Tennessee, 1869–1870.* Published Doctoral Dissertation, University of Tennessee.

Griffith, D. W., Dixon, T., & Triangle Film Corporation. (1915). *Birth of a nation*. Los Angeles, CA: Triangle Film Corp.

History.com Editors. (2018, August 29). *Ku Klux Klan*. Retrieved from HISTORY. https://www.history.com/topics/reconstruction/ku-klux-klan

Human Rights Watch. (1996). *Modern capital of human rights?: Abuses in the state of Georgia*. New York, NY: Human Rights Watch.

Jackson, H. A. (1973, November 8). Black mayor maps future of Atlanta. *Jet Magazine, 45*(7), 1–96. Retrieved From https://books.google.com/books?id= UrEDAAAAMBAJ&printsec=frontcover&source=gbs_ge_summary_r&cad=0#v= onepage&q&f=false

KKK group wants to preserve "our own slice of heaven" [YouTube Video]. (2015). Retrieved from https://www.youtube.com/watch?v=D1Qhd2ymtlA

Ku Klux Klan in the Reconstruction Era. (2000). Retrieved from New Georgia Encyclopedia. Retrieved from https://www.georgiaencyclopedia.org/articles/ history-archaeology/ku-klux-klan-reconstruction-era

Ku Klux Klan v. Martin Luther King Worshippers, 735 F. Supp. 745 (M.D. Tenn. –). (n.d.). Retrieved February 17, 2020, from Justia Law. https://law.justia.com/cases/ federal/district-courts/FSupp/735/745/1459533/

Langguth, A. J. (2015). *After Lincoln?: How the North won the Civil War and lost the peace*. New York, NY: Simon & Schuster Paperbacks.

Lewis, M., & Serbu, J. (1998). Kommermorating the Ku Klux Klan. *The Sociological Quarterly, 40*(1), 139–158. https://doi.org/10.1111/j.1533-8525.1998.tb02015.

Library of Congress. (1870). *Early KKK 1870*. Retrieved February 17, 2020, from Library of Congress. Retrieved from http://digitalexhibits.wsulibs.wsu.edu/exhibits/ show/reconstruction-416/item/4906

M.D Tennessee. (1990, April 19). *Knights of the Ku Klux Klan v. King*, 735 F. Supp. 745. United States District Court, Nashville.

Newbill, M. G. (1917, July). Birthplace of the Ku Klux Klan. *Confederate Veteran, 25*(7), 1–355. Nashville, TN: S.A. Cunningham.

Newton, M. (2014). *White robes and burning crosses?: A history of the Ku Klux Klan from 1866*. Jefferson, NC: Mcfarland & Company, Inc., Publishers.

Newton, M., & Newton, A. J.(1991). *The Ku Klux Klan?: An encyclopedia*. New York, NY: Garland.

Picciolini, C. (2018, January 27). He went to a KKK rally and stopped being a Violent Nazi Skinhead. *The Daily Beast.* Retrieved from https://www.thedailybeast.com/he-went-to-a-kkk-rally-and-stopped-being-a-violent-nazi-skinhead

Pinar, W. F. (2001). White women in the Ku Klux Klan. *Counterpoints, 163*, 555–619. Retrieved from https://www.jstor.org/stable/42977759

Pulaski Citizen [Pulaski, TN]. (1867a, April 19). *Chronicling America: Historical American Newspapers.*

Pulaski Citizen [Pulaski, TN]. (1867b, April 24). *Chronicling America: Historical American Newspapers.*

Pulaski Citizen [Pulaski, TN]. (1868, April 13).

Pulaski Citizen [Pulaski, TN]. (1917, May 1). Retrieved February 17, 2020, from Digital Collections. https://digital.lib.utk.edu/collections/islandora/object/volvoices%3A3865

Pulaski Citizen [Pulaski, TN]. (1985, January 21).

Pulaski Citizen [Pulaski, TN]. (1989a, September 5).

Pulaski Citizen [Pulaski, TN]. (1989b, October 3).

Pulaski Citizen [Pulaski, TN]. (1989c, October 10).

Pulaski Citizen [Pulaski, TN]. (1990, January, 9).

Riot against Negroes in Pulaski, Tennessee, 1868. (1868, January 9). *Nashville Union and American*, 3. Retrieved from https://www.newspapers.com/clip/28895736/riot_against_negroes_in_pulaski/

Robinson, M. A. (2017, December 28). *Pulaski, Tennessee race riot, 1868.* Retrieved February 17, 2020, from https://www.blackpast.org/african-american-history/pulaski-race-riot-1868/

Rothman, J. (2016, December 4). *The rise and fall of the second Ku Klux Klan.* Retrieved from The Atlantic. Retrieved from https://www.theatlantic.com/politics/archive/2016/12/second-klan/509468/

Sign the Petition. (2017). *Change.Org.* Retrieved February 23, 2020, from https://change.org/p/u-s-house-of-representatives-ban-the-kkk-rally-in-pulaski-tn

Sims, P. (1996). *The Klan.* Lexington, KY: Press of Kentucky.

Smith, L. (2018, February 21). *No, talking about women's role in white supremacy is not blaming women*. Retrieved February 23, 2020, from Medium. https://timeline.com/no-talking-about-womens-role-in-white-supremacy-is-not-blaming-women-f16739c46665

Travers, L. (2006). *Encyclopedia of American holidays and national days*. Westport, CT: Greenwood Press.

U.S. Census Bureau. (2018, December 6). *American community survey 5-year data (2009–2017)*. Retrieved from Census.gov. https://www.census.gov/data/developers/data-sets/acs-5year.html

White, J. (2000, May 20). *Former Klansmen indicted for murder in 1963 bombing of Birmingham, Alabama church*. Retrieved from Wsws.org. https://www.wsws.org/en/articles/2000/05/birm-m20.html

Willson, C. R. (1980). Front matter. In *Baptized in blood* (pp. i–vi). Retrieved from https://www.jstor.org/stable/j.ctt46nk5g

Chapter 5

THE STORY IN MONTANA

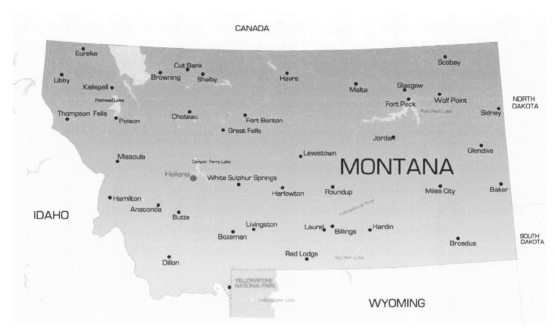

© Olinchuk/Shutterstock.com

OVERVIEW

While hate groups have been present in Montana since the 1920s, the Christian Identity movement moved in next door with the purchase of land in Hayden, Idaho by Richard Butler in 1973 (Kenna, 2014). In May of 1988, residents of Sanders County, Montana were concerned over the comments and actions of a recently arrived group of approximately 24 hard-core separatists. The group, comprised of Aryan Nations members, Constitutionalists, and Ku Klux Klan's (KKK) men had moved to the area with the intention of bringing their message of hate to Montana. In opposition to the group, a town hall meeting was held in the local Noxon High School gymnasium. The gathering drew a large crowd of 350 people (including approximately 50 protesting White separatists who gathered in the small rural county to hear stories from five members of the Kootenai County Task Force on Human Relations (KCTFHR) about how other communities had resisted White supremacist activity (Hult, 2016). At the end of the event, the attendees participated in four workshops and formed the Sanders County Task Force for Human Dignity (SCTFHD). While hate groups remain active in various Montana locations, the communities continue to find ways to support one another and live by the mantra "Love not Hate."

Timeline

1868	Fourteenth Amendment of the U.S. Constitution Was Adopted
1920	Ku Klux Klan Entered Montana
1960	Ku Klux Klan Reemerged
1973	Richard Butler Moved the Church of Jesus Christ Christian to North Idaho
1986	White Supremacists Declared Montana as One of the Five States of the "Aryan Homeland"; Pace Amendment Was Promoted at the Aryan Nations World Congress
1988	A Group of White Nationalists Moved to Saunders County, Montana; Kootenai County Task Force on Human Relations (KCTFHR) Talked to Concerned Saunders County Residents About Resisting White Nationalism; Sanders County Task Force for Human Dignity (SCTFHD) Was Created
1989	Montana State Legislature Passed Bill 293 Defining Hate Crimes as Malicious Intimidation or Harassment Relating to Civil or Human Rights
1990	Hate Crimes Increased Around the Country
1993	Residents across Montana Created Groups Based on Racial and Ethnic Equality to Respond to the Organized Hate Groups in the State
2010	KCTFHR Visited Montana to Speak at a Public Forum on How to Address White Nationalism
2010 to 2019	Communities Continued Various Responses to Hate in the State of Montana

BACKGROUND: SANDERS COUNTY, MONTANA, AND THE CHRISTIAN IDENTITY MOVEMENT

Montana, one of the Rocky Mountains states, is named for its mountainous regions. It is the fourth largest state by land mass, and is home Yellowstone National Park and Flathead Lake, the largest freshwater lake between the Mississippi River and the Pacific Ocean. UNESCO lists Glacier National Park as a World Heritage Site, protecting the park's plant and wildlife (History. com Editors, 2009). On average, Montana is populated with only six people per square mile, making it one of the country's least densely populated states. By 2030, Montana is expected to be ranked fifth in the nation in percentage of residents over the age of 65 (Montana Population, Demographics, Maps, Graphs, 2019). The social environment of the state of Montana has a high rating from U.S. News and World Report with high community engagement, social support, and voter participation (Abadi, 2018). At the same time, Montana has a very low equality score (#41) with a large income gap by gender and by race. From the years 2000 to 2010, there was a slight increase in the diversity of Montana, along with nearly a 10% growth in overall population (Montana Economic Report, 2019). It is reported that these changes were accompanied by increased dismay by some residents (Thackeray, 2012).

Located on the northwest border of Montana, Sanders County is almost 3,000 square miles in total. Sanders County remains sparsely populated with approximately 11,000 people (four people per square mile) and is moderately conservative, based on reports from the Pew Forum. According to the U.S. Census Bureau in 2018, people 25 or older with a minimum of a bachelor's degree composed 17% of the population, while at the same time, 20% of the people lived in poverty. People who identified as White alone, not Hispanic or Latino, composed 90% of the population. (U.S. Census Bureau Quick Facts: Sanders County, Montana, n.d.). At the same time, Confederate Salish and Kootenai Tribes make their home on over a million acres (approximately 1,500 square miles) of the Flathead reservation.

The natural landmarks of this rural community include two national forests and the Coeur d'Alene Mountains as well as the Clark Fork River, a tributary of the Columbia River (Clark Fork River United States, n.d.). Tufted duck and rough-skinned newt, as well as west slope cutthroat trout can be found in the waters. The redwing blackbird, Rocky Mountain bluebird, white-tailed deer, and black bear, along with wolves and cougars are some of the wildlife that can be found in the area. Ponderosa pine forests

© Patti Anderson/Shutterstock.com

are filled with huckleberry plants, a broad-leaf shrub that has not been domesticated (Sanders Country Montana Facts for Kids, n.d.).

With all of its resources and natural beauty, those attracted to the state include people who value less government interference, including tax protestors and sovereign citizens, and some who actively work to create a separate nation distinct from the United States of America. The KKK was drawn to the community and established a presence as early as the 1920s in several Montana communities, including Billings, Missoula, and Helena (Schontzler, 2017). The timing of the rise of the Klan coincided with the economic decline after World War I, when some people blamed financial strains on immigrants. At its height, Klan membership rose to more than four million people across the United States, targeting African Americans, Catholics, Jews, foreigners, communism, and organized labor (History.Com Editors, 2018). The Klan rose again in the 1960s in response to the Civil Rights Movement. The primary KKK tenant of the "purification" of American society continues with commitments to Christian Identity, among other supremacist ideologies (Ruker, 2009).

Using a religious argument (morality based on God's word) has been a powerful recruiting tool for White supremacist groups. According to the Christian Identity movement, the "lost tribes of Israel" populated the northern part of Europe creating Anglo-Saxon descendants; Christian Identity doctrine holds that Jewish people are the direct descendants of Eve and the serpent and people of color are considered to be "pre-Adamic" mud people who are a lower species than White people (McFarland & Gottfried, 2002). Christian Identity members range from passive believers to terrorists promoting race wars, using secret handshakes, code words, and initiation ceremonies to identify themselves. The Christian Identity movement was defined by a former Southern California Methodist Minister Wesley Swift who was active in extreme right-wing groups, including the KKK, linking the Christian Identity movement with extreme right-wing ideologies (Barka, 2006).

Richard Butler was a follower of Wesley Swift and moved Swift's Church of Jesus Christ Christian to northern Idaho in 1973 (Ludlow, 2001). It was in Hayden, Idaho that Butler created the neo-Nazi group Aryan Nations. Butler purchased 40 acres of land with the goal of uniting American hate groups for the purpose of creating a White Aryan nation (a Whites only republic) made up geographically from the states of Washington, Idaho, Oregon, Wyoming, and Montana (Barka, 2006). The Inland Northwest was targeted because there were few people of color living in the area, limited law enforcement, and a White population that was perceived to be apathetic to human and civil rights. The name "New Nation USA" with Missoula as the capitol was suggested. These efforts were highlighted during annual meetings ("congresses") held in Idaho (United States Commission on Civil Rights. Montana Advisory Committee, 1994). In 1985, James O. Pace (a.k.a. William Daniel Johnson) wrote a book advocating for the "Pace Amendment," which would repeal the 14th and 15th amendments and stated that only citizens would have the right and privilege to reside permanently in the United States (Southern Poverty Law Centre, William Daniel Johnson, n.d.). The Pace book included comments from Richard Butler. In 1986, Pace promoted the book by attending the Aryan Nations World Congress.

1986: RALLYING FOR THE DECLARATION OF INDEPENDENCE AND CONSTITUTION OF THE UNITED STATES

In the spring of 1986, there were several efforts to protest taxes in Montana. In Bitterroot Valley, protestors wanted to eliminate all property taxes in the state. A tax protest meeting was held in Noxon, a small town in Sanders County, followed by Bible studies that reportedly included conversations supporting the Christian Identity movement (United States Commission on Civil Rights. Montana Advisory Committee, 1994, pp. 14–15).

For over two years, local White supremacists, separatists, constitutionalists, and members of the Aryan Nation and the KKK spread information about their beliefs as a way to recruit new members. One of the tactics the groups used was writing letters to the editor in the *Sanders County Ledger*, the local newspaper. Because of its support for freedom of speech, the Ledger did not refuse to publish the letters despite increasing complaints that the newspaper was giving the groups too much space to share their hateful messages (Burris, Smith, & Strahm, 2000).

In the spring of 1988, a group of nationalists moved to Sanders County, Montana. Sanders County Sheriff James Doxtater estimated that there were approximately 24 members of the group. They represented membership in the KKK, Aryan Nations, and Constitutionalists. The 1988 letters to the editor in Sanders County had Constitutionalists themes. Constitutionalists purport that the U.S. Constitution and Bill of Rights were inspired by God and are morally binding, believing "we the people" refers to Christian White men as being innately (and exclusively) endowed with these rights. From this perspective, all other people are "14th amendment citizens," referring to the 14th Amendment of the United States Constitution (14th Amendment to the U.S. Constitution: Civil Rights (1868), 2015). The 14th Amendment was adopted in 1868 as a postcivil war Reconstruction Amendment, stating all persons born or naturalized in the United States and subject to the jurisdiction thereof, are citizens of the United States and of the state wherein they reside. Constitutionalists have a populist message, believing in equal rights for all depending on one's sex, race, religion, and ethnicity. Conspiracy theories espoused by Constitutionalists may also accuse Jewish people of controlling the Federal Reserve, international banking, and activities of the Internal Revenue Service (Jewish "Control" of the Federal Reserve: A Classic Anti-Semitic Myth, n.d.)

The publishing of letters continued unabated until the Spokane KXLY-TV Station ran a weeklong series focused on Sanders County. Five stories profiled prominent leaders of the Sanders County separatist movement, brought additional scrutiny to the groups and a shone a negative spotlight on Sanders County. The broader attention threatened Sanders' reputation and stood to impact tourist dollars and the ability to attract new residents and businesses.

In response to activities and statements by White supremacist groups, 350 to 400 Sanders County residents gathered in the Noxon High School gymnasium on Thursday, May 26, 1988 at 7 p.m. (Hult, 2016). Featured speakers at the event were five members of the KCTFHR from Idaho, only 100 miles west of Sanders County. Spokesman and Catholic

© haeryung stock images/ Shutterstock.com

Priest Bill Wassmuth, Tony Stewart, Norm Gissel, Marshall Mend, and Walt Washington shared their story of how their organization had formed to resist White supremacy in North Idaho. The KCTFHR was known nationally as a model for grass-roots efforts to combat prejudice and bigotry (About KCTFHR, n.d.). Marshall Mend commented "Saying yes to human rights is the best way to say no to prejudice" (Hult, 2016). "We all pray your experiences are not similar to ours; we don't want what happened to us to happen to you" said Stewart (Spokesman-Review, n.d.).

On May 26, the KCTFHR members were met at the Idaho/Montana state line by the Montana Highway Patrol to protect their safety. At the meeting, there were 11 Montana Highway Patrol officers plus members of the sheriff's departments from both Sanders and adjacent Lincoln counties (T. Stewart, personal communication, August 19, 2019). Law enforcement officers wore bulletproof vests to be prepared for potential violence. Approximately 40 to 50 protestors, identified with the KKK, the Aryan Nations, or the Posse Comitatus, also attended the rally to demonstrate on behalf of "White people" (Craft, 1994, p. 15). The supremacists carried signs, handed out literature, and some wore KKK shirts. They clapped every time a reference was made to White supremacy or separation. In response, the other residents applauded whenever there were messages of peace.

Tim McWilliams, a local high school teacher, presided over the program. The community rallied around support for the Declaration of Independence, all amendments to the Constitution of the United States, and Article 11, Section Four of the Montana Constitution, all of which support the dignity and equality of all persons (The Constitution of the State of Montana Preamble, n.d., p. 1087). The purpose of the meeting was not intended to stop or limit freedom of expression, but rather focus on a message of peace and human rights. Attendees participated in four workshops that evening culminating with the formation of the SCTFHD. It was a strategic move for the participants to break into four groups, each one focused on a specific town within the county to show the unity from each community: Noxon, Thompson Falls, Heron, and Trout Creek. Tony Stewart, leader of the KCTFHR noted that the four groups were "a wise move by the organizers and the people of Sanders County" (T. Stewart, personal communication, August 19, 2019).

The KCTFHR speakers were escorted back to the state line by the same law enforcement officers when the meeting was done. Although members of the task force had frequently been called to support communities addressing White supremacy, Tony Stewart of the task force said "it was one of the most tense and dangerous events that the KCTFHR has had excluding the 1986 bombings in Coeur d'Alene, Idaho" (T. Stewart, personal communication, August 19, 2019). Upon reaching home that evening, the speakers stopped to review the event and consider implications for the future.

With the formal creation of the SCTFHD, the intention was to model the new task force after the KCTFHR. Tim McWilliams was appointed the President and there was representation from each town in Sanders County. There was diverse representation in terms of color, religion, and political background. Members included religious figures, loggers, and educators. There was also a separate nonvoting advisory board comprised of state legislators, members of the police force, a school administrator, and the county attorney (The Spokesman-Review, 1988). The purpose of the SCTFHD was to provide a platform for people to speak to basic American values and promote legislation making malicious harassment because of race or religious beliefs a felony and subject to civil litigation (Minutes, 1989). They would also ask the legislature to treat paramilitary training as an act of terrorism.

POINTS TO PONDER

What were the initial efforts of residents of Saunders County residents in response to White nationalism in their community? How do you think your community would respond?

In early 1989, with testimony from residents, the SCTFHD, and others relating their experiences, the Montana Legislature passed legislation—Bill 293—defining hate crimes as malicious intimidation or harassment relating to civil or human rights (House and Senate proceedings, 1989). This legislation was intended to send a message to hate groups to avoid Montana.

1990s: FACT-FINDING AND LAW ENFORCEMENT

During the early 1990s, there was an increase in hate crimes across the country. People of color, Jewish people, and members of the lesbian, gay, bisexual, transgender, and questioning (LGBTQ) community, as well as Native Americans were often targeted (Rubenstein, 2004). On a Montana college campus in December 1991, the Church of the Creator advertised its newspaper, Racial Loyalty, as "dedicated to the survival, expansion, and advancement of the white race." It read, "White people awake! Save the white race—n_____, muds, and Jews-will be shipped out of the country" (Racial Loyalty, 1991). Racist literature continued to be distributed in Sanders County, too. In 1992 Bruce Barrett, a Missoula attorney, reported receiving three life threatening phone calls at his residence after giving a series of lectures on Judaism. Anti-Native America materials that opposed hunting regulations were distributed by All Citizens Equal (ACE).

In 1992, the Montana Advisory Committee to the U.S. Commission on Civil Rights, held a day-long fact-finding meeting to gather information on hate groups and their activities, legislation, and enforcement to counter hate groups, and uncovering supremacist goals to make the Pacific Northwest (Idaho, Montana, Oregon, Washington, and Wyoming) a "White republic."

During the Montana Advisory Committee fact-finding meeting, over 20 different active hate groups were identified, with most subscribing to racist, anti-Semitic, and anti-LGBTQ ideologies of Constitutionalists, Christian Identity, and or Christian Patriots, with some committed to anti-Native American and anti-government philosophies (Montana Advisory Committee, 1994). Those holding a Christian Identity theology claimed that their activities were for the purpose of establishing God's Kingdom on earth by a war in which Identity members are His (God's) instruments against satanic forces (Zeskind, The Christian Identity Movement, pp. 4246). As reported by the Advisory Committee, Black college students had been run off the road, told "the only good n_____ is a dead n_____," nearly hit by a truck while passengers laughed and shouted racial obscenities, and had a sign placed outside their campus housing saying "N_____ go home" (Montana Advisory Committee, 1994). Members of hate groups distributed literature, leaving it on parked cars during events organized by the Black Student Union. And by Holocaust denier Bradley Smith, appeared in the student newspaper at the University of Montana in Missoula.

Limited water resources are in part to blame for tensions between farmers and the Confederated Salish and Kootenai Tribes on the Flathead Reservation (Walker & Baker, 2013). Groups like the Montanans Opposed to Discrimination and the Citizens Rights Organization (Loesch,1993), believed the tribes were taking their water and anti-Native American sentiment was expressed in racists jokes, sports caricatures of Native Americans, name calling players "Kemosabe," parodied war whoops, and the "tomahawk chop."

The majority of hate crimes reported in Montana targeted the LGBTQ community, included beatings, threats of violence and death, verbal abuse, and the destruction of property. Specifically, fliers were distributed stating that the Bible prescribes the death penalty for homosexuals. An individual reported human feces smeared on the steering wheel of a truck with the lug nuts loosened, bricks thrown through the window of a house, and being assaulted and knocked unconscious in a busy downtown restaurant. Members of the LGBTQ community were particularly vulnerable to attacks by hate groups because they were not protected by the Civil Rights Act of 1964, the Governmental Code of Fair Practices, or the Montana Human Rights Act (United States Commission on Civil Rights. Montana Advisory Committee, 1994).

Again during the Montana Advisory Committee fact-finding meeting, Rick Day of the Montana Law Enforcement Services Division said that the state of Montana had one six-person unit to investigate hate crimes. Bill Alexander, Sanders County sheriff, stated that the 2,600 square miles of Sanders County were served by a sheriff's department with seven total deputies. Federal Alcohol, Tobacco, and Firearms agents provided three agents for the entire state.

> ## POINTS TO PONDER
>
> Why was there a rise of hate crimes in the United States during this time period? The case suggests that World War I and the Civil Rights Movement may have played a role in the surge of White nationalism in earlier time periods. What was occurring during the 1990s that could have been the context for another rise in hate crimes? The document presents that World War I caused a surge in White nationalism as well as the Civil Rights Movement. Was there anything like this that was going on during the 1990s that could have caused this to happen?

1993: THOUSANDS OF MENORAHS

In the 1990s, Montana residents took an active role in opposing the activities and visibility of organized hate groups across the state by forming local groups. These organizations included the Billings Forum on Racial and Ethnic Equality, the Flathead Reservation Human Rights Coalition, the Helena Human Rights Task Force, the Jocko Valley Coalition for Cultural Diversity, the Lincoln County Task Force on Human Rights, the SCTFHD, the Missoula Organization for Cultural Diversity, Out In Montana (the first statewide gay rights organization in Montana), and the Great Falls chapter of the National Association for the Advancement of Colored people. The Montana Human Rights Network was formed as a statewide organization to celebrate diversity and counter hatred, not as an intelligence gathering or data analysis group but rather to expose the philosophies of White supremacist groups and their operational and recruiting strategies (United States Commission on Civil Rights. Montana Advisory Committee, 1994).

To celebrate unity and Martin Luther King in January 1993, the Montana Association of Churches held an ecumenical service and organized a march in downtown Billings. After the event, participants found hate fliers on their windshields. This was followed by a Billings teenager being beaten with a baseball bat on March 1 by a gang of five, including at least one skinhead, who were racially motivated. In response, a rally called Stand Together, Billings! was held on May 2 at Rocky Mountain College. In mid-October, the home of a Native American family was spray-painted with racist graffiti and within days, the local painters' union and community volunteers repainted the home. The synagogue received a bomb threat just before the children's services on Yom Kippur and tombstones in the Jewish cemetery were desecrated. In addition, the conductor of the Billings Symphony and prominent member of the Jewish community, found a beer bottle tossed through the door of his home (Olp, 2013).

Then on December 2, 1993, a paving stone was thrown through a child's bedroom window that had been decorated with symbols of Hanukkah. Although the officers initially classified the crime as simple vandalism, the incident was seen as motivated by anti-Semitism and the local newspaper published a full-page color image of a menorah. People throughout the community placed the paper menorahs in their windows. The story was reported in the *New York Times* and made into a half-hour film that was aired on PBS in 1995 by Patrice O'Neill of The Working Group from Oakland, California. The film was titled *Not in Our Town* (Olp, 2013).

© Marina N. Mak/Shutterstock.com

POINTS TO PONDER

Imagine how difficult it must have been to be a racial/ethnic minority targeted by these hate groups during this time. Consider the courage it took for people to speak out against these forms of hate in the community while the hate groups were still very present. What would you have done if you experienced or witnessed someone being targeted by these hate groups?

THE WORK CONTINUES

In 1994, John Trochman and his brother formed the Militia of Montana and the United Citizens for Justice based out of Noxon. This was also the birthplace of the Church of the True Israel. Partly a response to Ruby Ridge, Trochman believed people should arm and prepare themselves in case the government came after them (Militias and Conspiracy Culture, 2013).

The year 2010 marked a time where some residents of Townsend would attend county commissioner meetings with the agenda of disruption using verbal attacks toward local politicians (Stewart, 2018). Letters of insult and injury would be written to the editor of the local newspaper, the *Townsend Star* (Hubber, 2018). Bill Hubber, a community activist of Townsend, reported that Tim Ravndal was one of the people who disrupted county commission meetings with anti-government rhetoric, emphasized ignoring federal gun laws, and thought of himself as a political operative (Hubber, 2018). After the meeting with Stewart and Gissel, the disruptions of commissioners meetings ended.

Ravndal loudly espoused marriage as a union only between a heterosexual male and heterosexual female and advocated for the Wyoming solution, a veiled reference to the horrific murder of Matthew Shepherd (Shahid, 2010). Ravndal held leadership positions in extremist groups such as Big Sky Tea Party where he formerly operated as president until he was fired for his LGBTQ positions (Shahid, 2010) and later served as Vice President for the Oath Keepers in 2015 (Alias, 2015). Big Sky Tea Party was an anti-government group featuring military heroes and freemen activist ideology (Hubber, 2018). The Oath Keepers group was based upon a philosophy of military and law enforcement that require members to sign an oath addressing one world government conspiracy theories of the anti-government movement (Montana Human Rights Network, 2011). The Sons of Liberty website (americanlibertyriders.ning.com) indicated that Ravndal was affiliated with additional groups, including the Montana Sons of Liberty, and the 2nd Amendment Group, as well as The 10th Amendment Center (Ravndal, 2013). The 10th Amendment Center declared that there are no federal rights, only states' rights. Ravndal was a part of creating a new political party, the Veterans' Party of Montana (Drake, 2015) and in 2018 after the failure of the Veterans' Party, he ran for office in the Montana House District 70 (For House District 70, 2018) where he was defeated by Republican, Julie Dooling (Kuglin, 2018).

In 2010, Hubber contacted Tony Stewart of the KCTFHR asking for advice on how to deal with the hateful newcomers in Townsend (Stewart, 2018). KCTFHR had a history along with recognition for creating successful strategies in dealing effectively with hate groups. The KCTFHR made the first of two visits on April 30, 2010 (Hubber, 2018). Hubber organized a county wide public forum with the support of both political parties in response to the presence of the hate groups (Stewart, 2018). The *Townsend Star* reported that Stewart and his colleague Norm Gissell presented ideas on how communities can stand up to hate groups, hate activities, and ways for community leaders to create unity and promote democratic ideals. Additionally, they also talked about effective ways to counter ethnic slurs and bullying behaviors (Human rights activists to speak in Townsend, 2010).

In Whitefish, Montana, the Jewish community in 2016 was about 60 people strong. The Whitefish Jewish community and allies were the target of aggressive troll storming and threats of violence orchestrated by neo-Nazi Andrew Anglin of the Daily Stormer and Richard Spencer. Spencer saw hate through an academic lens and emphasized a political route of rhetoric through media and speech. Anglin wanted actions such as an actual march with armed extremists and a possible revolt (Petersen, 2017). The situation in Whitefish arose over a real estate dispute between a Jewish realtor and Sherry Spencer, mother of Richard Spencer. Love Lives Here (LLH) was a campaign to counter the neo-Nazis actions and threats, operating similarly to the KCTFHR. LLH provided educational events and forums to promote peace and anti-hate resistance (Petersen, 2017) and would later become an affiliate of the Montana Human Rights Network. Rev. Darryl Kistler (pastor to the United Church of Christ) led the community with opposition protests toward the neo-Nazi presence in Whitefish (Petersen, 2017), accompanied by Rabbi Allen Secher and his wife Ina Albert.

© oatawa/Shutterstock.com

In January of 2017, the Whitefish community gathered for a "Love not Hate" rally in subzero temperatures to stand in solidarity against anti-Semitism. Community members from Whitefish and surrounding areas came together with food donations, a warming station and local media coverage. The Missoulian (2017) reported that Shaw, a member of the local community angered by the Nazi threats, believed that people should get outside and meet one another to overcome hate, and that's what the event was all about. In August of 2019, Anglin was ordered to pay the targeted Whitefish realtor $14 million for inciting the troll storm of hundreds of messages and calls. The following month, at the end of September, 2019, the Whitefish community found anti-Semitic fliers distributed, timed with Rosh Hashana events.

HEADLINE

Butte community holds rally in response to recent hate crime | ABC Fox Butte | montanarightnow.com

As of 2018, the Southern Poverty Law Center reported seven hate groups still active in Montana: Act for America (anti-Muslim), American Freedom Party (White Nationalist), Identity Evropa (White Nationalist), Last Chance

Patriots, (Anti-Muslim), National Policy Institute (White Nationalist), Pioneer Little Europe Kalispell Montana (White Nationalist), and Radix Journal (White Nationalist).

In 2019, the community rallied to support a resident with Native American ancestry whose home was painted with racist graffiti. Again, the community held a rally of support and a local business, Collins Painting in Butte, volunteered to repaint the neighbor's home for free. Community members raised money for security upgrades such as security cameras and motion lights for their neighbor's home (McCarthy, 2019).

DISCUSSION QUESTIONS

1.

Briefly describe the situation in the case. What aspects of your description are judgments (value statements about what is good or bad) and what aspects are objective statements?

2.

What do you think made Saunders County different from other communities that might have embraced White nationalism instead of speaking out against it?

3.

What methods were used in this case to address White nationalism? What strategies can you use that would work today?

4.

What goal(s) can you envision for the outcomes in this case? Brainstorm new strategies for reaching the goal(s). What are the strengths and limitations of each?

5.

What lessons do you take away from this case and how might you apply them in your own context?

REFERENCES

14th Amendment to the U.S. Constitution: Civil Rights (1868). (2015). Retrieved from Ourdocuments.gov, https://www.ourdocuments.gov/doc.php?flash=false&doc=43

Abadi, M. (2018, March 1). *The states where Americans have the best quality of life, ranked.* Retrieved February 28, 2020, from Business Insider. https://www.businessinsider.com/us-news-best-states-quality-of-life-ranked-2018-2

About KCTFHR. (n.d.). Retrieved March 2, 2020, from www.idahohumanrights.org, https://www.idahohumanrights.org/about.html

Alias, E. (2015, March 14). *Montana oath keepers meeting in Hamilton March 14 pb.* Retrieved July 2, 2018 from https://www.thepostemail.com/2015/03/14/montana-oath-keepers-meeting-in-hamilton-march-14-pb/

Barka, B. M. (2006). Religion, religious fanaticism and hate crimes in the United States. *Revue Française d Etudes Américaines, 110*(4), 107. https://doi.org/10.3917/rfea.110.0107

Burris, V., Smith, E., & Strahm, A. (2000). White supremacist networks on the internet. *Sociological Focus, 33*(2), 215–235. Retrieved February 29, 2020, from www.jstor.org/stable/20832076

Clark Fork River United States. (n.d.). Retrieved from Encyclopedia Britannica. https://www.britannica.com/place/Clark-Fork

The Constitution of the State of Montana Preamble. (n.d.). Retrieved from https://courts.mt.gov/portals/189/library/docs/72constit.pdf

Craft, M. V. (1994). *White supremacist activity in Montana.* Derby: Diane Pub Co.

Drake, P. (2015, September 17). *Veterans Party of Montana enters political arena. Great Falls Tribune: Part of the USA Today Network.* Retrieved from https://www.greatfallstribune.com

History.com Editors. (2009). *Montana.* Retrieved from HISTORY. Retrieved from https://www.history.com/topics/us-states/montana

Hubber, B. (2018, July 6). Phone interview with J. Dunbar.

Hult, K. (2016, May). *Fig Tree Kootenai County Task Force on Human Relations member, Marshal Mend, reflects on work.* Retrieved March 2, 2020, from www.thefigtree.org. https://www.thefigtree.org/may16/050116kctfhrmend.html

Human rights activists to speak in Townsend. (2010, April 15). Townsend Star.

Jewish "Control" of the Federal Reserve: A Classic Anti-Semitic Myth. (n.d.). Retrieved February 29, 2020, from Anti-Defamation League. Retrieved from https://www.adl.org/resources/backgrounders/jewish-control-of-the-federal-reserve-a-classic-anti-semitic-myth

Keenan, Catlyn Kenna, "Behind the Doors of White Supremacy". (2014). Electronic Theses and Dissertations, 329. Retrieved from https://digitalcommons.du.edu/etd/329

Kuglin, T. (2018, June 5). Montana primary: Helena-area legislative and PSC races. *Helena Air Independent Record*. Retrieved from http://helenair.com

Loesch, M. C. (1993). The first Americans and the "free" exercise of religion. *American Indian Law Review, 18*(2), 313. https://doi.org/10.2307/20068747

Ludlow, L. (2001, May 6). *Timothy McVeigh, an American patsy*. Retrieved February 28, 2020, from SFGate. Retrieved from https://www.sfgate.com/crime/article/Timothy-McVeigh-an-American-patsy-2923512.php

McCarthy, B. (2019, July 15). *Butte community holds rally in response to recent hate crime*. Retrieved February 29, 2020, from ABC FOX Montana. https://www.abcfoxmontana.com/butte/butte-community-holds-rally-in-response-to-recent-hate-crime/article_f2df0acc-8fd1-11e9-bf71-9b5e3a04369b.html

McFarland, M., & Gottfried, G. (2002). The chosen ones: A mythic analysis of the theological and political self-justification of Christian identity. *Journal for the Study of Religion, 15*(1), 125–145. Retrieved February 28, 2020, from www.jstor.org/stable/24764349

Militias and Conspiracy Culture. (2013, December 23). Retrieved February 29, 2020, from www.hate-speech.org. https://www.hate-speech.org/sovereign-citizens-militias-and-conspiracy-culture/3/

Minutes. (1989). *Montana house of representative 51st legislature—regular session committee on judiciary*. Retrieved from http://montanacourts.org/portals/189/leg/1989/house/03-09-hjud.pdf

Missoulian. (2017, January 7). *Hundreds rally in sub-zero temps to show love, not hate, defines Whitefish*. Retrieved from https://missoulian.com/news/local/hundreds-rally-in-sub-zero-temps-to-show-love-not-hate-defines-whitefish/article_78e7a29d-142e-55c1-a8eb-6d68386fd62e.html

Montana Advisory Committee. (1994). *White supermacist activity in Montana*. Montana Advisory Committee to the U.S. Commission on Civil Rights. US

Montana Economic Report. (2019). *2019 Montana economic report. Bureau of Business and Economic Research*. Retrieved from Bureau of Business and Economic. http://www.bber.umt.edu/pubs/Seminars/2019/EconRpt2019.pdf

Montana Human Rights Network. (2011, April 12). *Bozeman tea party promoting anti-government "patriots": Event features militia hero, freemen activist, and more* [Press release]. Retrieved July 2, 2018, from http://www.mhrn.org/publications/fact%20sheets%20and%20adivsories/Bozeman

Montana Population, Demographics, Maps, Graphs. (2019). Retrieved from Worldpopulationreview.com. http://worldpopulationreview.com/states/montana-population/

Olp, S. (2013, December 13). *A stone ignites a community: Billings stood up to white supremacists*. Retrieved February 29, 2020, from The Billings Gazette. https://billingsgazette.com/news/local/a-stone-ignites-a-community-billings-stood-up-to-white/article_1595787b-b44f-5a4f-b7b2-3a18e77615b7.html

Petersen, A. H. (2017, February 12). Love lives in whitefish, Montana, but so do Neo-Nazis. *BuzzFeed News*. Retrieved from https://www.buzzfeed.com/annehelenpetersen/love-lives-in-whitefish-but-so-do-neo-nazis?utm_term=.dl8b5XvAx#.byN4kdPx6

Racial Loyalty. (1991). *In internet archive*. Retrieved from https://archive.org/stream/RacialLoyalty_201704/Racial%20Loyalty%20-%20067_djvu.txt

Ravndal, T. (2013, March 8). *Not just "No," but "Hell No!"* [Web log post]. Retrieved from https://blog.tenthamendmentcenter.com/2013/03/not-just-no-but-hell-no/

Rubenstein, W. (2004). *The real story of U.S. hate crimes statistics: An empirical analysis*. Retrieved from https://williamsinstitute.law.ucla.edu/wp-content/uploads/Rubenstein-Hate-Crimes-Empirical-Analysis-2003.pdf

Ruker, P. (2009). *Rewind, leading into the sharp edges*. Retrieved from https://rewindexhibition.com/documents/PRucker_Rewind3_PressReady_rev1.pdf

Sanders Country Montana Facts for kids. (n.d.). *Kids encyclopedia fats*. Retrieved from https://kids.kiddle.co/Sanders_County,_Montana

Schontzler, G. (2017, September 17). *Bozeman's hidden history with the Ku Klux Klan*. Retrieved from Bozeman Daily Chronicle. https://www.bozemandailychronicle.com/

news/bozeman-s-hidden-history-with-the-ku-klux-klan/article_3b19194e-59a5-5ec5-9466-539d7c73774a.html

Shahid, A. (2010, September 7). Tea party president in Montana, Tim Ravndal, kicked out after posting anti-gay comments on Facebook. *New York Daily News*. Retrieved from http://www.nydailynews.com

Southern Poverty Law Center, William Daniel Johnson. (n.d.). Retrieved from Southern Poverty Law Center. Retrieved from https://www.splcenter.org/fighting-hate/extremist-files/individual/william-daniel-johnson

Stewart, T. (2018). *2010 & 2013 The Story of Townsend, MT*. Manuscript in preparation.

United States Commission on Civil Rights. Montana Advisory Committee. (1994). *White supremacist activity in Montana*. Denver, CO: U.S. Commission on Civil Rights, Rocky Mountain Regional Office.

U.S. Census Bureau QuickFacts: Sanders County, Montana. (n.d.). Retrieved February 28, 2020, from www.census.gov. https://www.census.gov/quickfacts/sanderscountymontana

Walker, S. A., & Baker, K-A. C. (2013). The confederated salish and kootenai tribes fight for quantified federal water rights in montana: A contentious history. *Journal—American Water Works Association, 105*(6), 12–16. https://doi.org/10.5942/jawwa.2013.105.0086

Chapter 6

THE STORY IN WYOMING

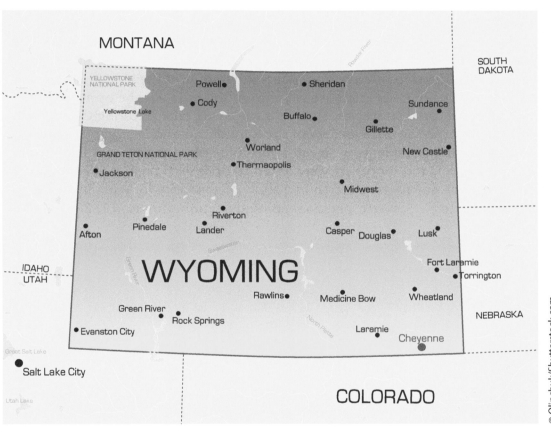

© Olinchuk/Shutterstock.com

OVERVIEW

In 1989 a special election was held to fill Wyoming's only seat the in the U.S. Congress when it was vacated by Congressman Dick Cheney, who resigned to become U. S. Secretary of Defense (Politics and National Issues, 1993). One of the candidates in the special election was William Daniel Johnson, who headed the Pace Amendment movement (Lazarus, 1989). The Pace Amendment proposed amending the U. S. Constitution to revoke the American citizenship of every non-White inhabitant of the United States (Aho, 1995, p. 261). In response to Johnson's candidacy, the opposing campaign adopted strategies, such as a statewide rally featuring Gov. Mike Sullivan and the key state leaders of the Republican and Democratic parties; having Wyoming residents wear red/white/blue ribbons each day leading up to the election, and motorists were asked to drive with their car headlights on during the day of the election in a show of solidarity for equality in the Equality State (T. Stewart, personal communication, August 19, 2019).

Timeline

1985	William Daniel Johnson Proposed the Ace Amendment
1986	The Aryan Nations World Congress Convened in Hayden, Idaho
1989, March	March Dick Cheney Resigned From His Position in the House of Representatives
1989, April	The League of Pace Amendment Advocates Announced It would Move to Casper, Wyoming; Johnson Ran as an Independent to Fill the Recently Vacated Seat in the Wyoming House of Representatives
1989	Tony Stewart, a Member of the Kootenai County Task Force on Human Relations (KCTFHR) and Kathy Karpan, a Member of the Northwest Coalition Against Malicious Behavior, Were Consulted Regarding Johnson's Campaign; Craig Thomas (R) Wins the Special Election
2006	Johnson Runs an Unsuccessful Campaign in the 8th Congressional District of Arizona
2008	Johnson Ran to be Elected as a Superior Court Judge in Los Angeles County, California
2009	Johnson and Other White Nationalists Created a New Political Party in California, the American Third Position (A3P).
2010	Johnson Spoke With the Southern Poverty Law Center About His Political Strategy for the American Third Position Party; The A3P Has Multiple Chapters Throughout the United States
2016	Johnson Recorded Robo-calls that Played in the States of Iowa, New Hampshire, Vermont, and Minnesota Promoting the Idea that the White Race Was Dying Out

BACKGROUND: WYOMING AND THE PACE AMENDMENT

The Rocky Mountains traverse the western two-thirds of Wyoming, the 10th largest state in the country. Almost half the land is owned by the U.S. government, including the Grand Teton and Yellow Stone National Parks (All About Wyoming, n.d.). Although bordered by six states, Wyoming is sparsely populated, with a total statewide population less than that of the neighboring city Denver (T. Stewart, personal communication, August 19, 2019). The culture of Wyoming is connected to its frontier heritage; the official state sport is rodeo, and its trademark symbol is a Bucking Horse and Rider (The complete guide to Wyoming, n.d.).

In 1985, attorney William Daniel Johnson of California proposed a constitutional amendment that would nullify the U.S. citizenship of every person of color in the America by repealing the 14th and 15th Amendments of the U.S. Constitution. William Daniel Johnson was born in 1954 and grew up in predominantly White neighborhoods in Arizona and Oregon until 1974, when he moved to Japan to study the Japanese language. While in Japan, Johnson talked about racial differences with people who were Japanese and began to embrace the idea that America's European heritage was at risk (Southern Poverty Law Center [SPLC], n.d.). Under the pseudonym James O. Pace, Johnson published *Amendment to the Constitution: Averting the Decline and Fall of America. In the book, he wrote* "We lose our effectiveness as leaders when no one relies on us or can trust us because of our nonwhite and fractionalized nature. . . [R]acial diversity has given us strife and conflict and is enormously counterproductive" (Pace, 1985).

The Pace Amendment proposed deporting all non-Whites, defined as people with an "ascertainable trace of Negro blood" or more than one-eighth "Mongolian, Asian, Asia Minor, Middle Eastern, Semitic, Near Eastern, American Indian, Malay or other non-European or non-white blood" (SPLC, n.d.). Positioning the amendment as protection for White Americans, non-Whites too old to bear children would have been exempted from deportation, while others would be paid to leave before a deadly "race war" could take place. For Johnson, the deportation of non-Whites was an act of self-defense, a preemptive strike in defense of real Americans (Blue, 2016). The League of Pace Amendment Advocates was organized in the early 1980s to support Johnson's efforts through legislation. Operating out of California, the league had a small staff that provided information and distributed materials (SPLCCenter, n.d.).

© Festa/Shutterstock.com

Richard Butler, founder of the Aryan Nations and Church of Jesus Christ Christian, endorsed Johnson's book Amendment to the Constitution: Averting the Decline and Fall of America. In 1986, the Aryan Nations World Congress convened in Hayden, Idaho for the purpose of supporting the separation of a White male dominated homeland in Washington, Oregon, Idaho, Montana, and Wyoming (Raab, 1988). Consistent with the premise of the Pace Amendment, Butler said "We're basically working toward a return to the kind of country our forefathers wanted when they came over on the Mayflower. You know yourself that today a white male is considered a third-class citizen by the de facto government, therefore, as the posterity of those who founded this country, it is our duty to reclaim our heritage" (Peterson, 1986).

Ku Klux Klan (KKK) members, Nazi sympathizers, White separatists, racists, and or anti-Semites went to the two-day Aryan Nations World Congress to hear speeches and see cross burnings. During the events, the perimeter of the compound was patrolled by men in camouflage carrying AR-15 automatic rifles. According to Butler, people came to the gathering because "they want to live with white people and educate their children with white people" (Peterson,1986).

Johnson attended the 1986 Aryan Nations World Congress. "The problem is that we have no discernment any more," he said, "we can't tell right from wrong anymore. We take a principle like free speech, which should be sublime, which is more than sacred, and turn it into a flood of pornography. It's as though we have forgotten how to reason" (Peterson, 1986).

POINTS TO PONDER

What made Butler claim that White men were third-class citizens? What was going on during this time to make him have this opinion?

1989: WYOMING'S SPECIAL ELECTION

By 1989, Johnson's reputation and relatively professional appearance convinced a group of White nationalists in Wyoming to encourage him to run for Congress, taking Dick Cheney's vacated seat in the U.S. House of Representatives (O'Donnell, 1989). Members of the U.S. House of Representatives are elected for two-year terms. House membership is apportioned by state according to population, with each state receiving a minimum of one representative (Encyclopedia Britannica, 2017). Wyoming, along with Alaska, Montana, North Dakota, South Dakota, and several states in the New England area only have one representative based on the populations in each state respectively (United States. Bureau of The Census, 1981). Cheney's political career included serving four Republican presidents and six terms in the U.S. House of Representatives, and culminated as U.S. Vice President to George W. Bush. On March 20, 1989, when Cheney resigned in order to fill his appointment by President George H.W. Bush to become secretary of defense (Cheney, 2014), the Wyoming seat in the U.S. House of Representatives opened up. Although Cheney was from Wyoming, Wyoming had no residency requirement for its seat in the U.S. House of Representative.

HEADLINE

"No Support" From Wyoming City: Glendale Group of White Supremacists May Move.

In April 1989, the League of Pace Amendment Advocates announced that it would move from California to Casper, Wyoming. First, an official resolution denouncing the group was issued by the Casper School Board. Later, the Assistant City Manager responded to the League relocation announcement by saying "They have not received any support here, and opposition to them has rallied around the issue of minority rights. I have to be cautious not to violate Mr. Johnson's civil rights, but I can say that he has no support here" (O'Donnell, 1989, p. 1). Additional political opposition came from Republican State Sen. Tom Stroock, "There's been plenty of evidence that Johnson's kind of thinking has no echo in a city like Casper with its tradition of independence and tolerance" (O'Donnell, 1989, p. 1).

Johnson ran as an independent candidate in the special election on April 25, 1989 for the Wyoming seat in the U.S. House of Representatives. Johnson had never run for political office before but when he moved to Wyoming, he collected 479 registered voter signatures to qualify as a candidate (SPLCCenter, n.d.). During his campaign, Johnson announced his White nationalist agenda. As reported by The Associated Press, Johnson said "Whites don't have a future here in this country, and that is . . . one of many issues that I am addressing" (SPLCCenter, n.d.).

John Abarr, a 19-year-old Klansman, ran Johnson's 1989 campaign. Abarr told a reporter that the KKK is "basically a civil rights organization that stands up for the rights of white people" (SPLCCenter, n.d.), just as the National Association for the Advancement of Colored People (NAACP) supports African Americans, Abarr framed the work of the United Klans of America as supporting the rights, pride and history of White people, with the purpose of creating a Whites only region in areas where there were already predominantly White populations, such as in Wyoming, Montana, Oregon, and Idaho. He recruited young people who were drawn to the Klan's robes and rituals like cross burnings and secret symbols and supported the Pacific Northwest as a home for Whites. "What I like to do is recruit really radical kids, then calm them down after they join" (Laura Zuckerman, 2013).

Tony Stewart and Wyoming Secretary of State Kathy Karpan were consulted regarding the special election and Johnson's campaign. Tony Stewart served as a leader in the Kootenai County Task Force on Human Relations (KCTFHR) in Coeur d'Alene, Idaho. Both Stewart and Karpan served on the Northwest Coalition Against Malicious Harassment (NWCAMH) Board (Humanrights.Org, n.d). At the time, Stewart was president of the NWCAMH and Karpan represented Wyoming Gov. Mike Sullivan on the NWCAMH Board.

The NWCAMH had been created in 1987 after the Aryan Nations' annual meeting near Hayden, Idaho the previous year. NWCAMH emerged from a human rights rally that was held in Coeur d'Alene, Idaho at the same time of the Aryan Nation 1986 meeting with the purpose of developing a mechanism to sustain efforts against hatred in the Northwest. The NWCAMH was formed as a nonprofit umbrella organization serving the states of Colorado, Idaho, Montana, Oregon, Washington, and Wyoming, working in partnership with human rights organizations, religious communities, law enforcement agencies, community groups, and organized labor. The governing board was composed of 37 members, representing the governor's offices in each of the five states as well as law enforcement and representatives from law enforcement, civil rights groups, and racial and ethnic minorities. The group increased awareness, community collaboration, and created a positive change in social climate through quarterly newsletters and an annual human rights conference (NWCAMH, n.d.). The NWCAMH was headquartered in Seattle, Washington with a staff of five people.

In this situation, Stewart and Karpan organized a statewide campaign to oppose Johnson's candidacy. During the statewide rally, members of both major political parties came together along with Wyoming Gov. Mike Sullivan (D). Stewart and Karpan coordinated the media campaign. Their message was to reject policies promoting hatred from the Johnson campaign and discourage Johnson's election. The campaign opposing Johnson's candidacy involved many strategies including having Wyoming residents wear red/white/blue ribbons each day leading up to the election. On Election Day motorists were asked to drive with their car headlights on (T. Stewart, personal communication, August 19, 2019). Johnson had gathered enough signatures to qualify for the ballot, however his election efforts were not successful.

Craig Thomas (R)	74,384	52.5%
John Vinich (D)	60,845	43.0%
Craig McCune (Libertarian)	5,825	5.8%
William Daniel Johnson	507	0.4%

Source: Special House elections, 1990.

© Rob Crandall/Shutterstock.com

The election results showed how successful the Karpen–Stewart campaign strategy had been in defeating yet another extremist movement. Considering Johnson had 479 eligible voters sign the paperwork to get him on the ballot and received 507 votes, he did not run a successful campaign. Craig Thomas, the winner of the House of Representatives election, went on to be reelected to the House in 1990, and again in 1992. In 1994, when his friend retired from the U.S. Senate, Thomas won election to take his place and was easily reelected in 2000 and in 2006, with over 70% of the vote. He was noted as one of Wyoming's most popular and beloved public servants. He died while in office of complications from leukemia (Senate Documents, 2007, pp. 101–102). "These efforts were some of the most successful initiatives of the KCTFHR since their founding" Stewart stated (T. Stewart, personal communication, August 19, 2019).

John Abarr continued his commitment to the Casper Area Skinheads, also known as the Wyoming Knights of the KKK. Johnson kept up his political work on a White nationalist platform although he was relatively inactive until 2006, when he unsuccessfully ran as a Democrat in Arizona's 8th Congressional district primary, campaigning to deport vast numbers of illegal immigrants and committing to fine and jail employers of illegal immigrants (SPLCCenter, n.d.). To bolster his campaign, Johnson brought in Russ Dove, an anti-immigration extremist with a felony conviction for attempted grand theft. Dove was also known for publicly burning a Mexican flag in April 2006 in Tucson. Johnson paid Dove more than $15,000 for "gathering signatures" and "consulting." But it was all to no avail. Johnson spent more than $133,000 of his own money but won only 2.9% of the vote (SPLCCenter, n.d.).

Johnson returned to California, where in September 2007 he hosted a $2,000-a-plate fundraiser at his ranch for the presidential campaign of U.S. Rep. Ron Paul (R-Texas). In June 2008, Johnson ran in a primary for Los Angeles County Superior Court judge. He avoided publicity, declining to respond to a questionnaire or give information about himself to the Los Angeles County Bar Association. But the Metropolitan News-Enterprise, a Los Angeles newspaper that covers law and the courts in detail, wrote a lengthy article about Johnson's background, including his role in promoting the Pace Amendment. Ron Paul then retracted an earlier endorsement of Johnson, who went on to lose the election with only 26% of the vote (SPLCCenter, n.d.).

In October 2009, Johnson met with members of Freedom 14, a racist skinhead group. Freedom 14 members created a new political party known as the American Third Position (A3P) and then renamed it the America Freedom Party (AFP) in 2013 (SPLCCenter, American Freedom Party, n.d.). Johnson was the group's chair and leading spokesperson. Kevin MacDonald, a California professor who believed that Jews destabilize the societies in which they live and are genetically programmed to attempt to out-compete non-Jews for resources, was also a leader in the group. "The Third Position insists that it is both healthy and divinely ordained that people should have a genuine love and preference for their own kind" (An Introduction to the American Third Position video, 2009).

POINTS TO PONDER

It was a strategic move for the League of Pace Amendment Advocates to move to Wyoming. As a result of Wyoming lacking a residency requirement to run for office, Johnson was able to run in the special election. What are the laws in your state regarding election residency laws? Could Johnson have done this in your state?

THE WORK CONTINUES

Speaking to the SPLC in January 2010, Johnson articulated his political strategy for the A3P party to run "high-level people" (prominent White nationalists) in state campaigns. In a radio interview on February 20, 2010, he stated: "The initial basis of our own upstart organization is the racial nationalist movement. It has been in disarray for the last 20 years." A3P recruiting materials use language such as "We of the Third Position look to the future and embrace principles that will secure the existence of our people and a future for our children." And "We need you to help us to secure the existence of our people and the future for our children." The language is similar to the "14 words" used by White supremacist David Lane.

The "14 Words" are based on content in Hitler's Mein Kampf: "We must secure the existence of our people and a future for White children." David Lane was imprisoned for his role in the 1984 murder of a Jewish talk show host in Denver. Later in March 2010, Johnson and his A3P cofounder, Kevin MacDonald, attended an event sponsored by the Institute for Historical Review, a Holocaust denial group (SPLCCenter, American Freedom Party).

The AFP "exists to represent the political interests of White Americans" and aims to preserve "the customs and heritage of the European American people." According to the SPLC, it is "arguably the most important white nationalist group in the country." In June 2010, A3P achieved the goal of active chapters throughout the United States, through a partnership of the Metro New York area chapter of the party. Johnson was active in promoting a new youth movement for 18- to 35-year-olds. As Johnson told the SPLC, "Our [AFP's] goal is to save the white race. Whatever approach works, we'll jump on that" (SPLCCenter, n.d.).

HEADLINE

'They don't need the baggage': White supremacist resigns as Trump delegate.

In 2016 before the Republican primaries, Johnson recorded robo-calls that were rolled out in Iowa, New Hampshire, Vermont, and Minnesota. During the calls, Johnson said "The white race is dying out in America and Europe because we are afraid to be called 'racist.' He forecast the "gradual genocide against the white race" and claimed that "few (U.S.) schools anymore have beautiful white children as a majority" (Sullivan & Elahe Izadi, 2016).

According to Johnson, the active campaigning and robo-call strategies helped the AFP find new members. The robo-calls included Johnson saying "My name is William Johnson. I am a farmer and a white nationalist" (Woolf, 2016). New members to the AFP reported that in the current political climate, they value "honest discourse" and feelings of being "emancipated." Johnson has also been active in promoting a new youth wing of AFP called the National Youth Front. Johnson also now finds it easier to be himself: "For many, many years, when I would say these things, other white people would call me names: 'Oh, you're a hatemonger, you're a Nazi, you're like Hitler'" (Jack, 2015).

DISCUSSION QUESTIONS

1.

Briefly describe the situation in the case. What aspects of your description are judgments (value statements about what is good or bad) and what aspects are objective statements?

2.

What strategies were used to discourage Johnson's campaign in the special election of 1989 in Wyoming? Were these effective? Could they be used today?

3.

How was Johnson able to run in multiple elections in varying states in his life? Although he was unsuccessful in winning an election, how did it impact the communities? Would you recommend that candidates be prevented from running or be allowed to run in elections in multiple jurisdictions? How would you operationalize your position (e.g., stricter elections residency laws in the case of the Wyoming special election)?

4.

What goal(s) can you envision for the outcomes in this case? Brainstorm new strategies for reaching the goal(s). What are the strengths and limitations of each?

5.

What lessons do you take away from this case and how might you apply them in your own context?

REFERENCES

Aho, J. A. (1995). *The politics of righteousness: Idaho Christian patriotism*. Seattle, Washington: University of Washington Press.

All About Wyoming. (n.d.). Retrieved February 27, 2020, from www.sheppardsoftware.com. http://www.sheppardsoftware.com/usaweb/snapshot/Wyoming.htm

An Introduction to the American Third Position [YouTube Video]. (2009). Retrieved from https://www.youtube.com/watch?v=znGozxcu6qc

Blue, M. (2016, January 11). *Man behind trump robocalls wants to deport non-Whites from U.S.* Retrieved from Right Wing Watch. https://www.rightwingwatch.org/post/man-behind-trump-robocalls-wants-to-deport-non-whites-from-u-s/

Cheney, D. (2014, April 2). Retrieved from Biography. https://www.biography.com/political-figure/dick-cheney

The complete guide to Wyoming. (n.d.). Retrieved February 27, 2020, from World Travel Guide. https://www.worldtravelguide.net/guides/north-america/united-states-of-america/wyoming/

Encyclopedia Britannica. (2017 June, 7). United States house of representatives seats by state. In *Encyclopædia Britannica*. Retrieved from https://www.britannica.com/topic/United-States-House-of-Representatives-Seats-by-State-1787120

Hensley, N. (n.d.). *Former KKK leader wants to reverse years of white supremacy by celebrating MLK Day in Montana*. Retrieved February 27, 2020, from nydailynews.com. https://www.nydailynews.com/news/national/kkk-leader-celebrate-mlk-day-montana-article-1.2485512

Humanrights.Org. (n.d.). Retrieved February 28, 2020, from www.idaho humanrights.org, https://www.idahohumanrights.org/history.html

Jack, F. (2015, October 27). *What?! LA county black probation officers hire white supremacist attorney* (EUR Exclusive). Retrieved February 27, 2020, from EURweb. https://eurweb.com/2015/10/27/what-la-county-black-probation-officers-hire-white-supremacist-attorney-eur-exclusive/

Laura Zuckerman. (2013, September 5). *Wyoming civil rights leader defends meeting with Klan*. U.S. Retrieved from https://www.reuters.com/article/us-usa-klan-wyoming/wyoming-civil-rights-leader-defends-meeting-with-klan-idUSBRE9840PZ20130905

Lazarus, B. (1989, March 30). *Backs whites-only citizenship: Glendale man runs in Wyoming*. Retrieved February 27, 2020, from *Los Angeles Times*. https://www.latimes.com/archives/la-xpm-1989-03-30-me-684-story.html

Northwest Coalition Against Malicious Harassment. (n.d.). Retrieved from clintonwhitehouse4.archives.gov, https://clintonwhitehouse4.archives.gov/Initiatives/OneAmerica/Practices/pp_19980803.17134.html

O'Donnell, S. (1989, April 14). "No support" from Wyoming city : Glendale group of white supremacists May Move. Retrieved February 27, 2020, from *Los Angeles Times*. https://www.latimes.com/archives/la-xpm-1989-04-14-me-1604-story.html

Pace, J. O. (1985). *Amendment to the constitution: Averting the decline and fall of America*. Los Angeles, CA: Johnson, Pace, Simmons, & Fennell.

Politics and National Issues. (1993). *Congress and the nation, 1989–1992, Vol. VIII: The 101st and 102nd Congresses* (pp. 6–27). Washington, DC: CQ Press. 10.4135/9781483302713.n1

Raab, E. (1988). Intergroup relations. *The American Jewish Year Book, 88*, 143–158. Retrieved February 27, 2020, from www.jstor.org/stable/23604149

Senate Documents. (2007). *United States Congressional Serial Set, Serial No. 15072*. 79the Congress, 2nd Session: United Stages.

Southern Poverty Law Center. (n.d.). *William Daniel Johnson*. Retrieved from Southern Poverty Law Center. https://www.splcenter.org/fighting-hate/extremist-files/individual/william-daniel-johnson

Special House elections. (1990). *CQ almanac 1989* (45th ed.). Washington, DC: Congressional Quarterly. Retrieved from http://library.cqpress.com/cqalmanac/cqal89-851-25635-1136836

Sullivan, K., & Elahe Izadi. (2016, May 11). They don't need the baggage: White supremacist resigns as Trump delegate. *The Washington Post*. Retrieved from https://www.washingtonpost.com/politics/trump-nominates-then-dumps-white-supremacist-as-a-gop-convention-delegate/2016/05/11/20281480-17a1-11e6-924d-838753295f9a_story.html

United States. Bureau of The Census. (1981). *1980 census of population and housing : Puerto Rico final population and housing unit counts*. Washington, DC: U.S. Dept. Of Commerce, Bureau of the Census.

Woolf, N. (2016, November 2). White nationalist halts robocall saying Evan McMullin is "closeted homosexual." *The Guardian*. Retrieved from https://www.theguardian.com/us-news/2016/nov/02/evan-mcmullin-robocall-closeted-homosexual-william-johnson

Chapter 7

THE STORY IN NORTH CAROLINA

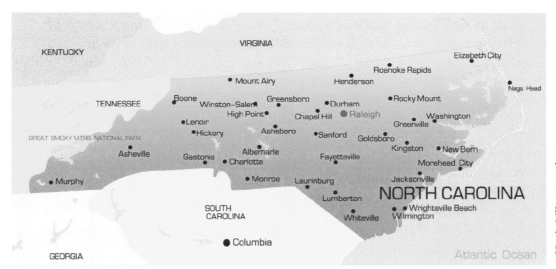

© Olinchuk/Shutterstock.com

OVERVIEW

In July of 1992, after the Southern Aryan Warriors and the Confederate Knights of America (CKA) distributed fliers in Buncombe County (Asheville; Gross, 1992b), several incidents involving the Ku Klux Klan (KKK), and an incident in which local resident Millard "Mitty" Owens became a victim of a racially motivated attack, Tony Stewart was invited by the Western North Carolina Citizens for an End to Institutional Bigotry (WNCCEIB), the Asheville/Buncombe Community Relations Council, and PRIDE (People Recognizing Individuality, Diversity, and Dignity in Everyone) to Asheville as a representative of the Kootenai County Task Force on Human Relations (KCTFHR) for two days of TV, radio, and newspaper interviews plus speaking at two public events. In response to these incidents, there was also an evening program at the YMI Cultural Center that included a showing of the 90-minute documentary by the KCTFHR titled "Stand Up to Hate Groups By Saying Yes To Human Rights" and a talk was held at the Black Mountain Presbyterian Church. On behalf of the KCTFHR, the three sponsoring human rights organization also received copies of the documentary to spread the message of tolerance.

Timeline

1988	The Confederate Knights of America Was Founded by Terry Boyce
1991	Southern Aryan Warriors and CKA Distribute Hate Fliers Throughout Buncombe County
1991	Kirk Lyons Declared as a National Leader in the White Supremacy Movement
1991	First Convention of the Western North Carolina Citizens for an End to Institutional Bigotry
1992	Lyons Establishes the CAUSE Foundation
1992, June	The "March for the Family and Traditional Family Values"
1992, July	Mitty Owens Was Attacked by Two White Supremacists
1992, July	Tony Stewart Visits North Carolina

BACKGROUND: WESTERN NORTH CAROLINA, THE CAUSE FOUNDATION, AND THE SOUTHERN LEGAL RESOURCE CENTER

North Carolina, one of the 13 original states, is located on the Atlantic coast. The region includes marshlands, coastal tidewater areas, and numerous lakes in addition to the Appalachian Mountains and urban centers. North Carolina was a part of initiating the Civil War as one of 11 states to secede from the United States (North Carolina, n.d.).

In the early 1990s, various White supremacy organizations expanded their presence and increased their activity in Western North Carolina, specifically in Asheville and the surrounding areas. Members of the KKK, Aryan Nations, Southern Aryan Warriors, and the CKA gradually increased their visibility and efforts to intimidate members of the community, while simultaneously recruiting White youth to join their ranks (KKK A History of Racism and Violence, 2011). Hate group activities included marching, distributing flyers with hate messaging, micro aggressions to normalize racial violence and breed a culture of fear through vandalism, making the call for leaderless resistance, filing lawsuits against the city, baiting victims/set-up situations to justify violence, and targeting key individuals in the community (Berger, 2019). Some of the hate groups prescribe to White supremacist religious ideology. Nord Davis, of the Northpoint Teams, published Christian Identity literature and a newsletter called "On Target." Davis, had been harassing the North Carolinians Against Racist and Religious Violence (NCARRV) and its executive director Christina Davis-McCoy. Nord Davis wrote literature criticizing Dr. Martin Luther King (MLK), Jr., dedicating it to Ms. Davis-McCoy in an effort to discredit her and NCARRV (QRD-NC Hate Crimes Report).

During 1991, the Southern Aryan Warriors and CKA distributed a high volume of fliers throughout Buncombe County including the city of Asheville, North Carolina. The CKA, also known as the National Socialist Front, was a neo-Nazi group, led by Terry Boyce of Huntersville, North Carolina. The CKA was founded in the winter of 1988, as a Klan splinter group that was "militant and violence-prone," said Mira Boland of the Anti-Defamation League (Masters, 1991). The group had a presence in prisons where inmates become hardened racists. Although not known at the time, John King who would be convicted of the 1998 violent lynching of James Byrd in Jasper, Texas, was the leader of the CKA—Texas Rebel Soldier Division (Croucher, 2019).

Kirk Lyons was described as a national leader in the White supremacy movement. The most prominent member of Lyon's family was his father-in-law Charles Tate, formerly second-in-command of the Aryan Nations compound in Hayden Lake, Idaho. Tate's daughter Brenna married Lyons at the Aryan Nations compound. Tate's other daughter, Laura, married chiropractor Neill Payne. Payne had a considerable criminal record and was affiliated with the Texas KKK and the Sons of Confederate Veterans (Southern Poverty Law Center, Kirk Lyons, n.d.). Payne and Lyons incorporated the Patriots Defense Foundation (PDF; Southern Poverty Law Center, Kirk Lyons, n.d.), which was a precursor to what would later become the CAUSE Foundation.

In early 1992, Lyons established a "pro-White law firm" named the Canada, Australia, United States, South Africa, Europe (CAUSE) Foundation in Black Mountain, 15 miles east of Asheville, North Carolina (Gilmour & Warren, 1994). CAUSE described itself as a "pro-White law firm" in an ad in Tom Metzger's White Aryan Resistance (WAR) publication and around this same time, there were numerous reports of skinheads assaulting African American teenagers and homosexual men (Gross, 1992b). Lyons would later cofound the Southern Legal Resource Center (SLRC), to defend neo-confederate culture and symbols. Klan and skinhead groups use Confederacy emblems as a statement of unity around racism and a continuation of treating people of color as inferior to Whites (Southern Poverty Law Center, Kirk Lyons, n.d.).

POINTS TO PONDER

Why do you think White supremacist organizations had to establish alternative organizations under different names in order to promote their cause? What does this indicate about the way ideas are spread and injected into society/a community? Are there any other contemporary organizations/centers/firms that you can think of that play a similar role in growing a movement?

In February 1992, residents of Buncombe County held a forum to discuss their growing concern about the local presence and activities of hate groups (Gross, 1992b), including increasing numbers of skinheads who had reportedly assaulted African American teenagers and gay men. A few different community organizations were formed in an effort to eradicate racism from the area. However, despite their focus and determination, over the next several months the rate of hate crimes continued to climb, and they questioned if their work was effective enough (Cabe, 1992).

The common pattern for White supremacy groups is to move into a community, keep a low profile, build up local support, and then become more active, according to Daniel Levitas (Gilmour & Warren, 1994), who is a national expert on White supremacy organizations and Executive Director of the Center for Democratic Renewal. When he met with Black Mountain community leaders in March 1992, he confirmed that a considerable number of internationally-connected and well-known White supremacists had settled in the area (Gilmour & Warren, 1994).

On June 20, 1992, several members from the various hate groups participated in the "March for the Family and Traditional Family Values," a parade organized by the community's conservative religious leaders (Blake, 1992). Many citizens felt threatened by the hate groups' public involvement in the parade and were anxious for the guidance and expertise Stewart could offer upon his upcoming visit (Gross, 1992a).

In order to maintain accreditation, the Asheville City Police created a specific position within department to focus on investigating the rapid influx of hate crimes. Within four months, Sergeant Bob Emory, coordinator of hate crime activity, investigated approximately 30 hate crimes including assaults, robberies, and vandalism. The majority of victims in these crimes had been targeted by the hate groups based on race, sexual orientation, religion, or gender (Gross, 1992b).

1990S: COMMUNITY VIGIL, ACCOUNTABILITY, AND HUMAN RIGHTS AS A PRIORITY

Mitty Owens was a YMI Community Economic Development Coordinator and he was physically attacked in Asheville, North Carolina because he is a person of color. Mitty, a graduate of Yale University and with a master's degree in community economic development, heard breaking glass near his home one July evening, and went outside to find out what was happening. He was taunted and punched by two skinheads (Gross, 1992b), testifying that the attacker said, "I'll teach you how to approach a white man." The community held a vigil in support of Owens that was attended by 100 citizens. The *Asheville Citizen-Times* reported on October 17, 1992 that the attacker was given the maximum two-year sentence under ethnic intimidation legislation. The sentence was the first conviction under the new Ashville hate crime code. Owens later said "The focus should be on instilling in people a sense of worth and accomplishment, of providing a measure of hope for the future" (Johnson, 1991).

The WNCCEIB first convened in 1991 to address racial discrimination in a local country club. They successfully campaigned the country club to change their by-laws to no longer prohibit African American and Jewish people from joining and to clarify women's membership standing following a divorce (Gilmour & Warren, 1994). The WNCCEIB continued to raise

© Maps Expert/Shutterstock.com

awareness about discrimination in the community and notified members of the community through public meetings and memoranda about ongoing hate. The WNCCEIB intentionally alerted the public to the habit of White supremacist groups becoming integrated into a community before revealing their true nature or intent and published memoranda detailing the people connected with Lyon (Gilmour & Warren, 1994).

HEADLINE

"The reality in Western North Carolina and across the country is that racism abounds in practically every institution. We do not need to be defensive about that fact. We need to do something about it."—Asheville Citizen Times, 05 Apr 1992, Page 29 - Asheville Citizen-Times at Newspapers.com

POINTS TO PONDER

Why is it important to understand the ways that White supremacist movements organize themselves and grow? Do you think that raising public awareness about the undercurrent nature of the movement is important at stopping its proliferation? Who is this information targeted toward—parents, schools, companies, activist organizations—and why?

The WNCCEIB's response was to Lyons and his "pro-White law firm" was to publicly declare that the community should not be seen as welcoming to White supremacists and instead "continuously and publicly promote our vision of a unified community that opposes white supremacist/separatist philosophy and teachings" (Gilmour & Warren, 1994). The group recommended community activities that promote unity such as The King Breakfast, art and essay contests associated with the Swannanoa Valley King celebrations, the Church Women United booth at the Sourwood

Festival, and a nine-week course, "Building Bridges: Overcoming Racism" held in Asheville. In addition, resolutions against hate crimes were passed by the town councils of Black Mountain and Montreat, the City Council of Asheville, and the Buncombe County Commissioners (Gilmour & Warren, 1994).

The WNCCEIB gathered information from now-unknown and unverifiable sources that Lyons spoke at various political rallies, extolling White supremacy, stating: "If we're going to succeed in a worldwide movement, for that of white rights and for whites' future, having a future at all, then we must encourage professionalism . . . the people are going to have to work in the political process and are gonna have to go back to basics. Get to the grassroots. How many of you asked someone from a high school to come with you today? . . . you've got to grab the young generation. I want to grab them before they get to law school so we'll have them" (Gilmour & Warren, 1998).

Joe T. Roy, chief investigator for the Klanwatch project of the Southern Poverty Law Center in Montgomery, Alabama, was quoted in the Raleigh News and Observer: "Lyons' language echoes the changing tone of white supremacists everywhere . . . They're becoming the kinder, gentler white supremacists." Ray continued to say "Their sales pitch is, 'I don't hate anybody; I just love the white race . . . I don't know if he's a card-carrying white supremacist, but you have to use your common sense. If it walks like a duck and talks like a duck, it's a duck" (Brown, 2008).

The WNCCEIB responded with the following statement:

> We in the Swannanoa Valley and Western North Carolina need to use our common sense and put it to work by public actions and deeds that affirm our commitment to equality, peace and harmony for all people. One question for us in the Swannanoa Valley and Western North Carolina is: How can we do more to ensure that young people in our communities have the thinking skills to ward off such "professional" deception? If there are those in our neighborhood who intend to divide this community along racist lines and who do not recognize the strength in diversity, then these people should be exposed for what they are. This organization intends to keep you advised of developments and continue to monitor activities of CAUSE and its members (Gilmour & Warren, 1994).

Meanwhile, on the other side of the country in Northern Idaho, the KCTFHR had produced a documentary, *Stand Up to Hate Groups by Saying Yes to Human Rights* to celebrate their 10th anniversary (North Idaho College, 1991). After requesting a copy of the documentary and watching the tactics employed by the KCTFHR, members of the Asheville community invited Tony Stewart, president of the KCTFHR, to return to his home state and share KCTFHR's methods of success in countering local hate groups (Cabe, 1992). Stewart was educated at the Western Carolina University and the University of Tennessee, and was a political science professor at North Idaho College.

During Stewart's visit on July 8 and 9, 1992, he participated in several events sponsored by the WNCCEIB, the Asheville/Buncombe Community Relations Council, and PRIDE. According to Mary Harayda, a member of PRIDE, his visit to Asheville was timely. Harayda said the presence of groups like skinheads, Aryan Nations, and the KKK, gave extra relevance to Stewarts appearance in Asheville. "We're still real concerned by those groups. (Some members) of the groups were marching in the Family Values Day Parade they're a threat," Harayda said (Gross, , 1992a).

HEADLINE

"Soft-spoken, gentle and eloquent, Tony Stewart is an unlikely trench warrior. Yet, by his own admission, Stewart, a native of Graham County, has fought an ongoing and vocal battle against hate groups in Idaho."— Asheville Citizen Times, 09 Jul 1992, Page 13 - Asheville Citizen-Times at Newspapers.com

Stewart came to share his expertise about how communities can best counter the efforts of White supremacist organizations in the area. He participated in a live interview on WLOS TV Noon News; gave a live interview on radio station WCQS 88.1 FM program called Conversation with host David Hurand; talked with Andy Gross, a staff writer for the *Asheville Citizen-Times*;

and attended a 7 p.m. program at the YMI Cultural Center that included showing of the 90-minute documentary by the KCTFHR, Stand Up to Hate Groups by Saying Yes to Human Rights (North Idaho College, 1991). On behalf of the KCTFHR, Stewart gave copies of the documentary to the organizations for further distribution. Stewart later gave an address to members of the African American community and he was honored with a reception. About 20 people, including two deputies from the Buncombe County Sheriff's Department, came to hear Stewart speak. Stewart said his impetus for battling hate groups came from a deceptively simple principle. "I have never understood why any individual would prejudge a person because of race, religion or color" (Gross, 1992a). On July 9, Stewart spoke to an audience at the Black Mountain Presbyterian Church. Stewart said of the trip, it was "One of the most rewarding trips on behalf of Human Rights."

Stewart stated that he believes the model to combat hate in Coeur d'Alene developed by KCTFHR is an example of a successful working model and is appropriate in Asheville (Cabe, 1992, p. 7). Stewart said the KCTFHR was formed after White supremacists groups in Idaho harassed a Jewish family and a multi-racial family in two separate incidents. The concerned people who came together in December 1980 to comfort a victimized Jewish neighbor has grown into a large group of people who have created a valuable coalition with clergy, law enforcement, educators, civic leaders, business leaders, elected officials, and the general public. According to Stewart, the group's activism and presence in Idaho helped law enforcement agents break up and arrest a dangerous group of White supremacists known as Order One (Gross, 1992a). Beside building coalitions designed to promote humanism and defeat unwarranted prejudices that fuel hate groups, Stewart said communities cannot engage in a conspiracy of silence when hate groups such as the Klan, Aryan Nations, or other White supremacist groups descend on a city. According to Stewart, "It's very important for any community that faces a problem with hate groups to recognize the threat and speak out. Hate groups don't go away because you wish them to go away" (T. Stewart, personal communication, August 19, 2019).

HEADLINE

"Hate flourishes when decent people do nothing, said the panelists at the hate crimes forum held at UNCA. Rather than react with indifference, people can combat hate through education, law enforcement, the courts, and community organizing."—*Ashville Citizen-Times*, 31 Oct 1992.

On October 18, 1997, about 25 Klan members from Surry County (100 miles east of Asheville), marched in Asheville (Gilmour & Warren, 1998). A Community Unity Rally was attended by hundreds in another part of the city, however, nearly 1,000 people countered the Klan downtown, with some throwing rocks and eggs to protest the marchers (T. Stewart, personal communication, August 19, 2019).

Robert Moore of Thomasville, North Carolina and "Grand Cyclops" of the American Knights of the KKK, applied for a rally permit to use a city facility. The permit was denied after Moore told the *Asheville Citizen-Times* in a December 23, 1997 interview that "It's going to be another Greensboro if they throw rocks" (Gilmour & Warren, 1998). According to a January 10, 1998 *Ashville Citizen-Times* article, Moore added to that comment saying "If they throw one rock, it won't take us but 88 seconds to wipe out what's standing across the street and God forbid if there's (sic) any children there" (Gilmour & Warren, 1998). He was referring to the 88 seconds it took Klansmen in 1979 to shoot down and kill five anti-Klan protesters in Greensboro, North Carolina. Moore also threatened the person who filed an injunction on January 8, 1998 to keep the KKK out of Asheville. Moore said in a January 10, 1998 *Asheville Citizen-Times* article: "She better keep her eyes open behind her head every day she walks down those streets" (Gilmour & Warren, 1998). WNCCEIB was able to secure a grant of $1,000 to pay for security measures for the individual who was threatened (Gilmour & Warren, 1998).

POINTS TO PONDER

Think about the role of violence in protest and counter-protest. Do you think the move to throw rocks/eggs at the Klan during the protest on October 18, 1997 in Surry County did more harm or good? Is there a role for violence in protest and counter-protest, and if so, how would you determine how far is too far? This can be further contextualized by modern day groups such as the anti-fascist protest movement, ANTIFA. Are groups like ANTIFA and those that use tactics that ANTIFA endorses important in the fight for human rights?

The WNCCEIB kept records of hate incidents and crimes, including a 1997 charges that the words "n_____ car" were scratched on vehicle, a 1997 cross burning outside a meeting to discuss forming a chapter of the NAACP, a 1997 unexploded pipe bomb at the home of a Jewish woman, a 1998 arson of a mixed racial couple's home, suspicions of KKK involvement in Rutherford County shooting at the home of an African American couple, and a 25 person Hendersonville 1998 KKK Rally (Gilmour & Warren, 1998). In 1998, a dead wild rabbit was found in the rural mailbox of the president of Citizens Against Discrimination, a group working for gay rights. The last "Update on recent Hate Activity in Western North Carolina including CAUSE, and other white supremacist/militia activity" report was in 1998 (Gilmour & Warren, 1998). In 2011, the group resumed a different type of publication switching to a newsletter.

THE WORK CONTINUES

Twenty years later, in October 2017, Michael Christopher Estes planted an ammonium nitrate and fuel oil bomb packed with nails and bullets in the concourse at the Asheville Regional Airport in North Carolina, saying to authorities that he was "preparing to fight a war on U.S. soil" (Carless &

Sankin, 2017). And during MLK celebrations in 2019, bags with weighted rocks were thrown onto yards, with recruiting fliers for the KKK and the group's phone numbers and a web address. "I would hope that Asheville as a community would stand against this nonsense, and put strong messages out and throughout North Carolina, and wherever that flyer came from, we will definitely resist that type of ignorance," councilwoman Sheneika Smith said (Kepley-Steward, 2019).

The SPLC has recorded 86 total incidents of hate in North Carolina during 2019, with most activity in leafletting (25 cumulative reports) and vandalism (27 cumulative reports) through November (T. Stewart, personal communication, August 19, 2019). The Anti-Defamation League's H.E.A.T. map (Hate, Extremism, Anti-Semitism, and Terrorism) collects data from sources including news and media reports, government documents (including police reports), victim reports, and extremist-related (ADL H.E.A.T. Map, n.d.). As of November 2019, the H.E.A.T. map indicated 94 incidents during 2018 to 2019. Most of these were White supremacist events or propaganda, with some Anti-Semitic incidents. Although North Carolina does have hate crime laws, the laws are noninclusive and do not address sexual orientation, disability, or gender identity (North Carolina, Out Leadership, n.d.).

The Asheville Buncombe Community Relations Council (ABCRC) was founded in the 1950s to support peaceful desegregation of area businesses, schools, and public facilities, with leadership from multiple professional and racial backgrounds. The group later engaged in issues of school integration and fair housing. And, the group was dissolved in February, 2016. The city and county decided to contract ongoing needs regarding discrimination, community education around issues of bias and discrimination, including training for law enforcement and community organizations, and others (Community Relations Council Dissolves, 2016).

According to their web presence as of November, 2019, WNCCEIB continues to provide assistance to victims of hate crimes; monitor activities of White supremacy, militia, and other hate groups in western North Carolina; assemble and distribute information about hate activity through printed publications and the Internet; address institutional discrimination/diversity issues with employers in the region in conjunction with workers of those institutions; and provide research, organizational assistance, and other support for communities and organizations faced with issues of hate activity and discrimination. On the 2016 newsletter of the WNCCEIB, they adapt Stewarts words, saying "Saying YES to Human Rights is the best way to say NO to racism and bigotry" (WNCCEID, 2016–2017, p. 8).

DISCUSSION QUESTIONS

1.

Briefly describe the situation in the case. What aspects of your description are judgments (value statements about what is good or bad) and what aspects are objective statements?

2.

Tony Stewart—founder of the Kootenai County Task Force—is a White man. Do you think his positionality, related to his identity, has influenced the way he addresses hate and bigotry throughout different communities? Do you think his racial identity as a key figure in the fight against White supremacy is important? Why or why not?

3.

List multiple stakeholders in the case and identify the actions/strategies that each took. Why did each stakeholder (Terry Boyce, Kirk Lyons, the Confederate Knights of America [CKA], Mitty Owens, the Western North Carolina Citizens for an End to Institutional Bigotry [WNCCEIB], Asheville Buncombe Community Relations Council [ABCRC], etc.) choose a particular strategy and what criteria did they use to determine what actions would be the "right" actions to take?

4.

What symbols, language, celebrations, stories, practices, and so on are used by each stakeholder to communicate what their group thinks is important and guides the behaviors of the group? Pay special attention to who the groups were emphasizing as important demographics.

5.

Who were the key leaders? Describe their roles and how they influenced other people to support their strategies. How did Tony Stewart influence the way that movements against hate were instigated in North Carolina? Do you think the emphasis on human rights was effective in efforts to combat hate? Why or why not? Do you think there are more effective strategies, and if so what would they be?

6.

What goal(s) can you envision for the outcomes in this case? Brainstorm new strategies for reaching the goal(s). What are the strengths and limitations of each?

7.

What lessons do you take away from this case and how might you apply them in your own context?

REFERENCES

ADL H.E.A.T. Map. (n.d.). Retrieved from Anti-Defamation League. https://www.adl.org/education-and-resources/resource-knowledge-base/adl-heat-map

Berger, J. M. (2019, August 7). *The strategy of violent white supremacy is evolving.* Retrieved March 2, 2020, from The Atlantic. https://www.theatlantic.com/ideas/archive/2019/08/the-new-strategy-of-violent-white-supremacy/595648/

Blake, B. (1992, 19 June). Preaches on parade: Religious leaders plan family values march. *Asheville Citizen-Times.* Retrieved from http://www.newspapers.com/image/200152377/?terms=Family%2BValues%2BDay%2BParade

Brown, T. (2008). Shame, honor, and denial in the symbolic ethnicities of southern whites. *Safundi, 9*(3), 291–309. https://doi.org/10.1080/17533170802172917

Cabe, A. (1992, 20 July). *North Carolina turns to N. Idaho: Stewart teaches anti-hate tactics.* Couer d'Alene Press. Retrieved from https://issuu.com/molsteadlibraryatnic/docs/kootenai_county_task_force_on_human_63fcdb9a1a0341/24

Carless, W., & Sankin, A. (2017, November, 17). *The Hate Report: He was "preparing to fight a war on US soil".* Retrieved March 2, 2020, from Reveal. https://www.revealnews.org/blog/hate-report-3-men-3-bombs/

Community Relations Council Dissolves. (2016, March 31). Retrieved March 2, 2020, from Buncombe County Center. https://www.buncombecounty.org/countycenter/news-detail.aspx?id=16169

Croucher, S. (2019, April 20). *James Byrd Jr. Killer faces imminent execution.* Retrieved from Newsweek. https://www.newsweek.com/james-byrd-jr-lynching-texas-death-row-execution-1394474

Gilmour, M., & Warren, B. (1994, February). *Western North Carolina citizens for an end to institutional bigotry.* Retrieved from https://www.main.nc.us/wncceib/94whole.htm

Gilmour, M., & Warren, B. (1998, Summer). *Update on recent hate activity in western North Carolina including cause, and other white supremacist/militia activity.* Retrieved from https://www.main.nc.us/wncceib/98whole.htm

Gross, A. (1992a, July 9). Speaker tells of long fight against Idaho hate groups. *Asheville Citizen-Times.* Retrieved from http://www.newspapers.com/image/201742462/?terms=%22Tony%2BStewart%22

Gross, A. (1992b, July 24). Police still investigating alleged beating. *Asheville Citizen Times*. Retrieved from http://www.newspapers.com/image/201747566/?terms=Millard%2BOwens

Johnson, P. (1991, November 24). *Group seeks rebirth of south pack*. Retrieved from http://www.newspapers.com/image/?spot=21656664

Kepley-Steward, K. (2019, January 21). *Asheville Police investigating after reports of KKK flyers being found in area*. Retrieved March 2, 2020, from WLOS. https://wlos.com/news/local/asheville-police-investigating-after-reports-of-kkk-flyers-being-found-in-area

Ku Klux Klan A History of Racism and Violence. (2011). Retrieved from https://www.splcenter.org/sites/default/files/Ku-Klux-Klan-A-History-of-Racism.pdf

Masters, B. A. (1991, August 10). Racist fliers credited to KKK turn up in fairfax. *Washington Post*. Retrieved from https://www.washingtonpost.com/archive/local/1991/08/10/racist-fliers-credited-to-kkk-turn-up-in-fairfax/b29b7218-5e51-4908-9ea7-560f7f98241b/

North Carolina. (n.d.). Retrieved March 2, 2020, from Encyclopedia Britannica. https://www.britannica.com/place/North-Carolina-state/Climate

North Carolina, Out Leadership. (n.d.). Retrieved March 2, 2020, from https://outleadership.com/states/north-carolina/

North Idaho College (Producer). (1991). *Stand up to hate groups by saying yes to human rights: 1981–1991*. [YouTube]. Available from https://www.youtube.com/watch?v=J5sPQMQeco8

Southern Poverty Law Center, Kirk Lyons (n.d.). Retrieved from Southern Poverty Law Center. https://www.splcenter.org/fighting-hate/extremist-files/individual/kirk-lyons

Western North Carolina Citizens for An End to Institutional Bigotry. (2016–2017, Winter). Retrieved from http://wncceib.org/wp-content/uploads/2014/05/WNCCEIB-NL16.pdf

Chapter 8

THE STORY IN PENNSYLVANIA

© Olinchuk/Shutterstock.com

OVERVIEW

A July 29, 2002 Pittsburgh Tribune-Review article by Anne Michaud described a growing concern about extremists moving to Pennsylvania, stating "A faction of the Aryan Nations intends to establish a national headquarters in Potter County, north of State College, and hosted a three-day rally this weekend that drew more than 100 Nations members, Posse Comitatus followers, skinheads, Klansmen and hate rock bands" (Michaud, 2002a). Community leaders, including David Shtulman with the American Jewish Committee in Pittsburg invited members of the Kootenai County Task Force on Human Relations (KCTFHR), Marshal Mend, Norm Gissel, and Tony Stewart, for a week-long tour of Pennsylvania with several state and national officials in human rights, government, and law enforcement. The intervention strategy included speeches with public audiences, private lunches and dinners with local leaders, media interviews and strategy sessions with a number of groups sharing the message: "Never, never take the position that because there are a few of them, they will do no harm. Reacting once in a while will not keep the community safe. Please never remain silent . . . Please commit your life to the dignity of others" (T. Stewart, personal communication, August 19, 2019).

Timeline

1992	Ex-Klansman and Minister in the Christian Identity Movement Moves to Potter County
1994	Threats and Harassment Targeting an Interdenominational Coalition of Preachers
2002, July	Three-Day Aryan World Congress
2002, July 29	*Pittsburgh Tribune-Review* Reports on Extremist Movement Coming to Potter County

BACKGROUND: PENNSYLVANIA, A NEW ARYAN NATIONS HEADQUARTERS, AND THE ARYAN WORLD CONGRESS

The state of Pennsylvania is filled with open skies and outdoor activities. At the very northern part of the state, Potter County is close to the New York State border and is surrounded by forest land. Home to the Pennsylvania Grand Canyon, the Pine Creek Rail Trail, other attractions including mills and music festivals, the community has a rural, small town feel (PA Grand Canyon—Lodging, Attractions, Directions, Maps, n.d.). The forests are home to bald eagles, deer, bear, fox, and turkey as well as other migratory birds and rainbows, browns and native brook trout swim in rivers and streams. With the Allegheny National Forest to the west, the Susquehannock State Forest directly south, and the Tioga State Forrest to the east, an Aryan headquarters would be very well protected from outsiders. Local reporter, Dennis Roddy, referred to the area as, "a gorgeous range of forested mountains and tidy, small towns along the Pennsylvania-New York border" (Roddy, 2002b).

In 2002, the Aryan Nations started the move to Pennsylvania due to infighting in the organization. Splinter groups emerged to separate from Richard Butler, who founded the Aryan Nations in Southern California after World War II

© MH Anderson Photography/Shutterstock.com

(Southern Poverty Law CenterCenter, Aryan Nations, n.d.). Richard Butler was first introduced to the Posse Comitatus, a group known for anti-military activities and he attended a Christian Identity Church that taught that Whites are the real Israelites and Jews are descended from Satan (Southern Poverty Law Center, Richard Butler, n.d.). Butler eventually became an ordained minister in this church. While working for Boeing, he was introduced to the Pacific Northwest where he eventually decided to establish his vision for a White homeland. In 1973, Butler moved to Hayden, Idaho, formed his own church and eventually the Aryan Nations, to spread a pro-Hitler hate message. Butler continued to grow his organization, becoming a leader among the various White supremacist groups (Ku Klux Klan: A History of Racism, 2011). He hosted events and drew people to his Northern Idaho location. Before too long, Butler's group became connected to a crime spree. Butler was not derailed from his activity until a civil case brought by the Keenan family and the Southern Poverty Law Center resulted in bankruptcy in 2000. After losing the legal battle, the group headed by Richard Butler was in financial trouble. At this same time, Richard Butler also started to have his own health difficulties. Between the financial troubles, and Butler's physical deterioration, the Aryan Nations organization was in decline (Southern Poverty Law Center, Richard Butler, n.d.). The bankruptcy was also the instigation for the splinter groups to separate and start their own organizations. It was during this time that August Kreis decided to start the Aryan Nations in Pennsylvania determining to set up a compound in Potter County (Southern Poverty Law CenterCenter, August Kries).

POINTS TO PONDER

What do you think is causing conflict within the in-group of this hate organization? How is religion being used for/by leadership within the hate organization? Leadership here is sophisticated and driven by motivations of power. Richard Butler is an educated engineer and represents leadership for this hate organization, yet struggles in terms of leadership status and power achievement. Why?

The segment of the Aryan Nations moving their new planned headquarters to Potter County, Pennsylvania was headed by August Kreis III and Ray Redfearin (Roddy, 2002a). In Spring of 2002, the new location would be ready for the leadership and new direction. August Kreis, an ex-Klansman and self-taught minister in the Christian Identity Movement, had moved to Potter County in 1992. The town of Ulysses was made up of one main street, a U.S. Post Office, a funeral home, and lots of trees. While Kreis had an Aryan Nations web site that invited followers to move to whiter and brighter Potter County, the only new arrivals were children he fathered with his common law wife and Joshua Caleb Sutter, a leader in this faction of the Aryan Nations (Roddy, 2002b). His messages also played on people's fears of government overreach, which "tramples their constitutional rights to free speech and freedom of assembly, and that the government, media, businesses and financial institutions are manipulated by Israel" (Michaud, 2002b). Kries points to the police presence at their events as evidence that the government is trying to take their rights away.

Kreis had a history of illegal activity to gain income for himself. He defrauded the government by pretending to be a Veteran in order to claim Veteran's benefits (Southern Poverty Law CenterCenter, August Kries). He was eventually caught, ordered to repay the money, and imprisoned for the crime. Kreis used religion to justify and legitimate his activities through references to its "biblical" nature. In 1994, Kreis began a six-year campaign of threats and harassment targeting an interdenominational coalition of preachers in Potter County (Southern Poverty Law CenterCenter, August Kries). The preachers had come together to publicly oppose his views and activism. Kreis on several occasions showed up at meetings of Potter County United, videotaping the proceedings and threatening to "bring in Ku Klux Klan (KKK), neo-Nazis, and skinheads." He boasted of secret cross burnings and proclaimed, "I'm recruiting your kids" and other threats through repeated answering machine and e-mail messages (Southern Poverty Law CenterCenter, August Kries).

Led by Kreis, the Aryan Nations promoted the "whiteness" of Potter County and advertised it as a place for White people (Worden, 2002). This strategy not only encouraged the relocation of more like-minded people, but it also discouraged anyone else from wanting to live in the area. Real Estate agents were challenged with showing property in the area, knowing that it is against the law to discriminate, yet the followers of Kreis were advertising and encouraging White people to move to Potter County to live among other White people (Worden, 2002).

HEADLINE

"I don't want even the slightest influence of that organization in the county where I live. I don't think most of the people of Potter County are going to fall for the influence of a group like Aryan Nations." Rev. Doug Orbaker, pastor of First Presbyterian Church in Coudersport. The Buffalo News—January 30, 2002. Unwelcome Guests the Hate Group Aryan Nations Plans to Set Up its New Headquarters in Ulysses, Pa., A Two-Hour Drive from Buffalo, and Residents Aren't Happy About Their New Neighbors

---

After settling into the small town of Ulysses, Pennsylvania, the Aryan Nations hosted a three-day Aryan World Congress at the end of July 2002 (Anti-Defamation League, 2013). The gathering was attended by skinheads, Klansmen, neo-Nazis, and White power bands, totaling about 100 people who paid $35 each to camp on land owned by Kreis. They listened to bands with names like Intimidation One, Max Resist, and White Wash. Kreis engaged James Wickstrom, a longtime Identity preacher who worked with White supremacy leaders like Gordon Kahl of the Posse Comitatus and members of The Order, a neo-Nazi group that was involved in bank and armored car robberies and the shooting murder of a Jewish talk show host in Denver. With the success of this event, the Aryan Nations had loudly announced its presence (Suall & Lowe, 1987).

POINTS TO PONDER

In other case studies, we have learned that a lot of White supremacists groups try to hide the nature of their cause and keep a more low-profile status in the community. What makes this situation different? What risks does this open up for the community and the White supremacist group?

Meeting with the media during the gathering were Wickstrom, Kreis, Sutter, and Aryan Nations leader Charles Juba. According to Wickstrom, hate is healthy because it is biblical and the world is run by Jews who manipulate African Americans and other minorities. He spoke admiringly about The Order and its violent path while Kreis promised that synagogues and mosques in America would be burned down. He went on to say someday professional golfer Tiger Woods and his White (then) girlfriend would be beheaded. The local community quickly realized that this group could become a significant threat to the area and community leaders began to get concerned (Roddy, 2002).

2002: THE COMMUNITY RESPONDS

On July 29, 2002, a local reporter for the *Pittsburgh Tribune-Review*, Anne Michaud, wrote a column about the growing concern of an extremist movement coming to Potter County. She raised awareness of the emergence of a faction of the Aryan Nations who was planning on making a national headquarters in the northern part of Pennsylvania (Michaud, 2002a). The reporter provided background of the activity of the Aryan Nations and their activity in the state of Idaho. Marshall Mend, a cofounder of the KCTFHR, expressed concern with the increase in skinhead activity in Pennsylvania. With humor, he apologized, explaining that he did not realize that when they kicked the Aryan Nations out of Idaho, that they would land in Pennsylvania. With years of experience dealing with the Aryan Nations, several members of the KCTFHR offered to assist Potter County, Pennsylvania in their efforts to counter hate. With the alert issued, and the history and context provided in the local newspaper (Michaud, 2002b), the community took note of this hate group and initiated a plan of action. It was newspaper reporter Anne

Michaud's article that became the pivotal moment causing concerned leaders to reach out to the KCTFHR.

On July 29, 2002, a local reporter for the *Pittsburgh Tribune-Review*, Anne Michaud, wrote a column about the growing concern of an extremist movement coming to Potter County. She raised awareness of the emergence of a faction of the Aryan Nations who was planning on making a national headquarters in the northern part of Pennsylvania (Michaud, 2002). The reporter provided background of the activity of the Aryan Nations and their activity in the state of Idaho. Marshall Mend, a cofounder of the KCTFHR, expressed concern with the increase in skinhead activity in Pennsylvania. With humor, he apologized, explaining that he did not realize that when they kicked the Aryan Nations out of Idaho, that they would land in Pennsylvania. With years of experience dealing with the Aryan Nations, several members of the KCTFHR offered to assist Potter County, Pennsylvania in their efforts to counter hate. With the alert issued, and the history and context provided in the local newspaper, the community took note of this hate group and initiated a plan of action (Michaud, 2002). It was newspaper reporter Anne Michaud's article that became the pivotal moment causing concerned leaders to reach out to the KCTFHR.

Community leaders, civil rights groups, and others invited members of the Kootenai County Task Force to visit the state of Pennsylvania. David Shtulman of the Pittsburgh Chapter of The American Jewish Community was chosen to arrange the visit of the KCTFHR representatives. A week-long tour included private lunches and dinners, media interviews, speaking events by Mens, Gissel, and Stewart in cities across Pennsylvania and strategy sessions (Michaud, 2002b). Immediately upon the arrival of the Kootenai County Task Force, a law enforcement group was attached to the tour. This sent a message to anyone paying attention that the task force had the support of law enforcement.

POINTS TO PONDER

How does a community get law enforcement involved, when the citizens view law enforcement as an illegitimate organization? Is getting law enforcement involved always the best option?

The task force members on the tour included Marshall Mend, Tony Stewart, and Norm Gissell. They provided guidance while touring the state. The schedule of the task force members involved public presentations, media interviews, and private meetings starting at the University of Pittsburgh with about 100 people in attendance. They told all those in attendance about their experience dealing with the Aryan Nations. They provided a stern warning to take the arrival of this group seriously (Michaud, 2002a). As is typical of Stewart's approach, each community across the state was asked to be creative and come up with customized solutions. He urged members of each community to be creative and thoughtful in their response   (Iacone, 2012). Simply, KCTFHR advised the communities to not remain silent in the face of this invasion of a hate group (Michaud, 2002a). Stewart told those in attendance at the University of Pittsburg that the KCTFHR made a mistake early on regarding the Aryan Nations in Hayden, Idaho believing that because the group was so small that it was benign. "Never, never take the position that because there are a few of them, they will not do harm." Reacting once in a while will not keep a community safe. "Please, please never remain silent. Please do not confine yourselves to a counter-rally, and please commit your life to the dignity of others" (Michaud, 2002a).

The KCTFHR Pennsylvania tour included events at the University of Pittsburgh (William Pitt Union) sponsored by the American Jewish Committee; at Greensburg and Westmoreland County sponsored by the Young Women's Christian Association (YWCA) and Westmoreland County Unity Coalition; at Coudersport and Potter County sponsored by Potter County Unity Coalition and the Gospel Tabernacle Church; at York/Lancaster sponsored by the Social Justice Committee of the Unitarian Church and the York City Human Rights Commission; and at Boyertown and Berks County sponsored by Reading/ Berks Human Rights Commission and Boyertown Unity Coalition. The week's tour ended in Philadelphia.

Some of the organizations that were represented for all or part of the week's tour included the Pennsylvania Highway Patrol, the United Jewish Federation, the Federal Bureau of Investigation (FBI), the U.S. Department of Justice Community Relations Service, the Pennsylvania state legislature, the Pennsylvania Attorney General's Office, the University of Pittsburgh's Institute of Politics, the U.S. Department of Housing and Urban Development, the Pennsylvania Human Rights Commission, and the Pittsburgh Chapter of the

American Jewish Committee. "Since the founding of the KCTFHR, the July 2002 Pennsylvania tour involved more organizations and governmental units by far than any other community or state visit in which we have participated" said Stewart (T. Stewart, personal communication, August 19, 2019).

> ## HEADLINE
>
> "I think our job as a community is not to prevent Mr. Kreis or anyone else from living here, but to communicate firmly the values upon which our country rests. Those are tolerance and respect for our neighbors no matter what their race, creed or color."- Joseph Wolf, pastor of St. Paul's Lutheran Church. Buffalo News.

One member of the community implemented his own strategy. Michael Reid infiltrated the Aryan Nations group in Potter County and became a resource for information about the group. He gained knowledge about the capabilities of the group in terms of weaponry. He knew what types of guns they had and how many they owned (Michaud, 2002b).

The Potter community also created the Potter County United coalition of churches for the purchase of training and education materials for key stakeholders in the Potter and Tioga County school districts (Michaud, 2002). The Aryan Nations tends to try to recruit young people, so partnering with schools was a good strategy, and one often suggested by the KCTFHR.

THE WORK CONTINUES

Pennsylvania has a long history of hate group activity and reported more hate crimes as compared to other states (Iacone, 2012). It should be noted that the state of Pennsylvania is one of the states that does report hate crimes, while some states do not report hate crime activity at all and so caution is needed in interpreting this data. Pennsylvania can clearly track the presence of 32 White supremacist groups in 71 communities and two Black supremacist groups. The police in the state of Pennsylvania reported 43 hate crimes during the years of 2010 and 2011 (Iacone, 2012).

According to Barry Morrison, the Philadelphia based regional director for the Anti-Defamation League, "The Aryan Nations has remained in a weakened state and has had trouble attracting followers and had problems with succession in its leadership." In August of 2016, the neo-Nazis were back in Potter County. The National Socialist Movement (NSM) of Pennsylvania, a Whites only political organization, planned to meet in or around Ulysses on August 13, 2016. The goal stated by Steve Bowers, NSM of Pennsylvania leader, is to turn Pennsylvania into a stronghold of White supremacy (Stemcosky, 2016). The group planned a Swastika lighting at dusk according to the movement's website, because the Swastika represents the White race. Bowers claimed the group did not advocate any kind of violence "because it is just self-defeating and stupid" (Gettys, 2016).

At the same time as the event planned by Bowers, area residents are planning to counteract the meeting with a peaceful protest, with one resident saying that, "we cannot allow this element into our county," Joe Leschner, who organized the peaceful protest dubbed the Potter County Anti-Racism Rally, wanted to "show these misguided Americans that Potter County and North Central Pennsylvania does not share their views. And more personally to show my wife and all immigrants that the majority of white America supports them and stands with them against racism" (Davis, 2016). Mark Pitcavage, Anti-Defamation League official discouraged people from disrupting the meeting because people could get hurt and it might only serve to give the White supremacists free publicity. He reminded people that the region didn't have many NSM members and therefore the NSM rally attendance would be small. If the local community wanted to demonstrate its opposition to the sentiments of a neo-Nazi group like the NSM, he recommended organizing a unity rally or celebration somewhere else, to give a positive message (Davis, 2016).

HEADLINE

"Our country needs people to unite it, not divide it. It needs more cooperation and understanding, not hate and anger."—State Rep. Martin Causer, who represented most of Potter County. Bradford Era. August 2, 2016. Neo-Nazi group plans event in Potter County

DISCUSSION QUESTIONS

1.

Briefly describe the situation in the case. What aspects of your description are judgments (value statements about what is good or bad) and what aspects

2.

What are the signs of a hate group emerging (or existing) within a town/city?

3.

Acts of crime by a hate group are violence, robbery, murder and so on. What purpose(s) does such acts of crime serve for the hate group?

4.

What goal(s) can you envision for the outcomes in this case? Brainstorm new strategies for reaching the goal(s). What are the strengths and limitations of each?

5.

What lessons do you take away from this case and how might you apply them in your own context?

REFERENCES

Anti-Defamation League. (2013). *Aryan Nation/Church of Jesus Christ Christian*. Retrieved from Anti-Defamation League. https://www.adl.org/sites/default/files/documents/assets/pdf/combating-hate/Aryan-Nations-CJCC-Extremism-in-America.pdf

Davis, A. (2016, August 2). *Neo-Nazi group plans event in Potter Co.* Retrieved March 2, 2020, from Olean Times Herald. http://www.oleantimesherald.com/news/here_and_now/neo-nazi-group-plans-event-in-potter-co/article_15871d28-58bf-11e6-bddc-b7d6284ce05d.html

Gettys, T. (2016, August 2). *'Bring the kids': Neo-Nazis plan picnic to make Pennsylvania county a white supremacist hotbed again*. Retrieved March 2, 2020, from www.rawstory.com. https://www.rawstory.com/2016/08/bring-the-kids-neo-nazis-plan-picnic-to-make-pennsylvania-county-a-white-supremacist-hotbed-again/

Ku Klux Klan: A History of Racism. (2011). Retrieved from Southern Poverty Law Center. https://www.splcenter.org/20110228/ku-klux-klan-history-racism

Lacone, A. (2002, May 13). Communities urged to combat hate activity. *Pittsburgh Tribune Review*. Retrieved March 2, 2020, from https://triblive.com/x/pittsburghtrib/news/westmoreland/s_83904.html

Michaud, A. (2002a, July 22). Idaho Group warns of racism. *Pittsburgh Tribune Review*. Retrieved March 2, 2020, from https://triblive.com/x/archive/1714086-74/archive-story

Michaud, A. (2002b, July 29). *Pittsburgh tribune-review*.

Michaud, A. (2008, August 3). Extremist maintain PA presence. *Pittsburgh Tribute Review*. Retrieved March 2, 2020, from https://triblive.com/x/pittsburghtrib/news/regional/s_85102.html

PA Grand Canyon—Lodging, Attractions, Directions, Maps. (n.d.). Retrieved from pacanyon.com. https://pacanyon.com/

Roddy, D. (2002a, June 29). *Aryan Nations moving to state*. Retrieved from http://old.post-gazette.com/headlines/20020129aryans0129p5.asp

Roddy, D. (2002, July 28). *Aryan Nation shares its message of hate*. Retrieved from http://old.post-gazette.com/nation/20020728arayans2.asp

Southern Poverty Law Center, Aryan Nations. (2010). Retrieved from Southern Poverty Law Center. https://www.splcenter.org/fighting-hate/extremist-files/group/aryan-nations

Southern Poverty Law Centre, Richard Butler. (n.d.). Retrieved March 2, 2020, from Southern Poverty Law Center. https://www.splcenter.org/fighting-hate/extremist-files/individual/richard-butler

Stemcosky, K. (2016, August 10). *National Socialist Movement holding meeting in Ulysses*. Retrieved March 2, 2020, from TiogaPublishing.com. http://www.tiogapublishing.com/potter_leader_enterprise/news/national-socialist-movement-holding-meeting-in-ulysses/article_27682536-5e74-11e6-a46a-f3965103b181.html

Suall, I., & Lowe, D. (1987). The hate movement today: A chronicle of violence and disarray, Terrorism. *Taylor & Francis Online*, 10(4), 345–364. https://doi.org/10.1080/10576108435692

Worden, A. (2002). *Neo Nazi cells call Whites to ponder county*. Retrieved March 2, 2020, from https://www.stormfront.org/forum/t12473/

Chapter 9

THE STORY IN OREGON

OVERVIEW

Scotta Callister, editor of the weekly *Blue Mountain Eagle* newspaper in John Day, Oregon called the Kootenai County Task Force on Human Relations (KCTFHR). She had interviewed Paul Mullet, a neo-Nazi, who was in the city to announce his attention to purchase property in Grant County and establish a new Aryan Nations' headquarters and compound. Tony Stewart and Norm Gissel were invited to visit John Day for a full day of activities with the residents of the county to discuss strategies on how to deal with the threat of a neo-Nazi presence. Two public rallies, a press conference, and a private luncheon with city and county leaders as well as meeting various local residents was scheduled. Green ribbons were purchased and placed in all the storefront windows, on cars, and people were observed wearing the ribbons. Nearly 40% of the county's 7,500 residents viewed the rallies either in person or by streaming them. *The Oregonian* newspaper in Portland quoted Stewart's opening remarks from the evening rally: "Tonight I declare victory for you. When you come together as one people and one voice and built a wall of unity, no hate can penetrate that wall."

Timeline

2004	Richard Butler Dies and Paul Mullet Stakes His Claim to the Title of Leader of the Aryan Nations
2010, February 17	Paul Mullet Came to John Day to Propose Relocating the Aryan Headquarters There
2010, February 26	Norm and Diana Gissel and Tony Stewart Visit John Day to Discuss With the Community How to Organize Against Hate
2010, February late	Paul Mullet Relocated to Chillicothe, Ohio

BACKGROUND: JOHN DAY, OREGON, AND MULLET'S ARYAN NATIONS

John Day, Oregon is located in Grant County. It is a gorgeous part of the country, home to John Day Fossil Beds National Monument, Painted Hills, and the John Day River. According to Kathie Stoddard, a real estate agent, "This is paradise" (Associated Press, 2010). The nearest major cities are Portland, Oregon, which is located about 200 miles away and Boise, Idaho, almost 150 miles away. John Day is a rural community with a population of about 2,000, with only 7,000 residents in the 4,500 square miles of the entire county. In the midst of land covered with forests, county unemployment in 2010 was the highest in the state at 16% and the population was aging as younger members of the community left in search of employment. However people in the community choose to live there both because of the natural beauty as well as the communal aspect of everyone knowing each other's names in the small town setting.

The mayor affirmed that the community is strong and that people stand in solidarity when they are threatened (Associated Press, 2010). This was tested when Paul Mullet came to John Day on February 17, 2010 looking to purchase an old junior high school, a vacant church, and/or an opera house. Mullet handed out business cards and wore a uniform shirt with a swastika patch on it. He told the *Blue Mountain Eagle* local newspaper that "We're here in town and we just want to let you know what's going on," said Scotta Callister, editor (Aney, 2018). Mullet wanted to start a soup kitchen for the community, as well as a training facility, barracks, and site for national gatherings of the Aryan Nations, with the first one planned for September, 2011. His purpose was to create a national headquarters and homeland for White people. "That area is the Pacific Northwest," he said. "The blacks have Africa, the Jews have Israel . . . " (White supremacists eye property in John Day, 2010).

Mullet, from Athol, Idaho, identified himself as the national director of the Aryan Nations. His claim to national leadership stemmed from the 2004 death of Richard Butler, the founder of the Aryan Nations in Hayden, Idaho. Butler's Aryan Nations was bankrupted by a civil suit in 2000, resulting in many followers leaving the group and forming multiple factions in Idaho, New York, Ohio, Missouri, and other states (Southern Poverty Law Center, Paul Mullet, n.d.). The judgment in the civil suit was $6.3 million including the rights to the "Aryan Nations" name for a mother and son who were attacked by guards of Butler's compound. According to Tony Stewart, a human rights activist who helped represent the attacked family, the winning plaintiffs "could go to court and refuse to let any faction of the Aryan Nations use that particular name in the future." August Kreis III of St. Cloud, Florida also claimed he was the true Aryan Nations leader. "I don't even know who Paul Mullet is," said Kreis, 55. "There's a bunch of idiots up there in Idaho" (Cockle, 2010).

Mullet's Aryan Nations headquarters at the time was in Athol. The website of the group promoted an all-White "state," with its own government and military. The remote qualities of Grant County, in addition to the low cost of property and mountain terrain would have provided an ideal setting for a training ground for survivalists in his mind. When asked about the source of funds to purchase real estate, Mullet commented that he would pay cash "from legal means" (Southern Poverty Law Center, Paul Mullet, n.d.).

Jacob Green and Christopher Cowan, Grant County residents, along with Leif Berlin, accompanied Mullet while he was in John Day. Green, was the Aryan Nation's Oregon state leader, and Cowan was described as a sergeant in the state organization (White supremacists eye property in John Day, 2010). Berlin was described as a state leader from Washington on the group's website. As with Butler's former compound in Hayden, Idaho, the group's website featured Nazi materials and at the same time claimed not to be a hate group. "This is a good fit with the values here," Mullet said. He claimed members would do community service projects and patrol the streets, making it safer for the residents who lived in John Day. He also claimed that having the Aryan Nations in the community would bring money to the economy by drawing more supporters to visit and live in the area. "Coming here would help the county immensely," Mullet said (Callister, 2010a).

While staying at a local motel, Mullet and those accompanying him opened the door to their room to clearly display Nazi-style banners while an African

American and Hispanic employee were in the vicinity. According to motel personnel, guests in two rooms terminated their stay because they did not want to stay where White supremacists were staying (Callister, 2010a).

FEBRUARY 26: "NO HATE. NO ARYAN NATIONS. NO NEO-NAZIS. GOD MADE EVERYONE"

After Scotta Callister, editor of the John Day weekly *Blue Mountain Eagle* newspaper, made the strategic move to interview Paul Mullet and publish the interview along with a photo of him displaying his neo-Nazi uniform, much of the entire county was alarmed. Callister's decision became the pivotal moment for action. The *Blue Mountain Eagle*, had a weekly circulation of 3,500. Callister was a lifelong news professional who moved to Grant County three years earlier from the Portland area. She knew how important a small newspaper was, providing local news and acting as a watchdog for the community. Callister noted that she would have difficulty with a position "neutral to a hate movement" (Associated Press, 2010). In less than a week, three Grant County Facebook groups opposing the Aryan Nations sprang up, with a total of almost 5,500 members. A 20-year resident by the name of Stoddard ran off extra copies of a flier created by her 12-year-old child, who was passing them out on John Day's main street. The flier read: "No hate. No Aryan Nations. No neo-Nazis. God made everyone." (Associated Press, 2010).

HEADLINE

"The outcry was immediate following an article in the local newspaper, the *Blue Mountain Eagle*. The paper sponsored two informational meetings to inform local residents about the Aryan Nations beliefs and activities."— *Blue Mountain Eagle*, Town Unites Against White Supremacist Group

© Billion Photos/Shutterstock.com

POINT TO PONDER

Paul Mullet informed the local newspaper when he got there which enabled Callister to write her article and begin the push against his movement. Do you think the results of the John Day organizing would have been different if the media/Callister's response was delayed? How does media and the way news is employed influence the way that movements grow? Is it against journalistic ethics to lean into one's bias on a topic? Where is should the line be drawn between social/moral/community obligation and the objectivity of the press?

Callister called Norm Gissel, attorney and board member of the KCTFHR, seeking information and advice on how to proceed. After several conversations with Callister, Norm Gissel with additional task force members Tony Stewart and Diana Gissel were invited to visit John Day to discuss strategies with the residents on how to deal with the threat of the neo-Nazi presence (History, n.d.). Callister and Marissa Williams, the *Blue Mountain Eagle* publisher, organized the day's itineraries that included two public rallies, a press conference, and a private luncheon with city and county leaders as well as meeting various local residents (Stewart & Gissel, 2012).

On February 26, the first event of the day was a Friday morning rally at 9:00 a.m. at the community center in Canyon City, near John Day. There was an overflowing crowd that exceeded 350 people (Fire laws limited attendance to 300 in that space). An additional 150 people were turned away and told to return for a later event Friday evening. Stewart and Gissel spoke that morning for an hour followed by an hour of audience questions. At 11:00 a.m. the two men held a press conference with regional and national journalists and TV reporters. In his message, Tony Stewart said "What you've all done is spoken with one voice, and there's no way hate can penetrate that kind of unity" (Associated Press, 2010).

At the private luncheon, a detailed discussion was held with 20 community leaders that included office holders, educators, law enforcement, business leaders, faith community, youth, editor and publisher of the newspaper, and representatives of both political parties. It was decided at the luncheon that those present would establish a Grant County Human Rights Coalition with the mayor of John Day as the interim chair. That afternoon, about 100 people waved signs discouraging the Nazi presence at the town's only stop light, and drivers passing by honked their horns. Townspeople gathered at the main square holding signs of support for human rights. Green ribbons were

© PPstock/Shutterstock.com

purchased and placed in all the storefront windows, cars, and log trucks and people were observed wearing the ribbons in solidarity (T. Stewart, personal communication, August 19, 2019).

At the 6:00 p.m. community hall rally once again there was an overflow crowd with everyone wearing a green ribbon plus a large green wreath hung from the podium. People had to once again be turned away due to space constraints. Once again Stewart and Gissel gave an hour's presentation followed by an hour of audience questions. In a session streamed live on the local newspaper's website, one resident after the other was emphatic: The Aryan Nations was not welcome in their community. The final tally indicated that nearly 40% of the county's 7,000 residents viewed the rallies either in person or by streaming them. The gatherings represented all segments and regions of the county's population (T. Stewart, personal communication, August 19, 2019).

Many residents did everything they could to let the Aryan Nations know they were not welcome in John Day. Main street businesses put signs in their windows stating they have the right to refuse service to anyone. Other signs read "No Nazis" and "No Aryan Nations" (Small Oregon town rallies against Aryan Nations, 2010), residents felt that even the threat of the White supremacist group coming to town was hurting business. As an example, a motorcycle club that held an annual rally in the town said they wouldn't continue to do hold their rally in the community if the Aryan Nations moved in. Norm Gissel said the neo-Nazi movement had a chilling effect on tourism and property values in northern Idaho during its heyday under Richard Butler. When Gissel was asked about Mullet's group going to Grant County, Gissel said, "From an economic standpoint alone, you don't want that to happen in your community. You've got a potentially serious problem, and the time to start organizing is right away" (Callister, 2010a).

HEADLINE

"The community rallied with signs and letters and forums to educate residents and thwart the potential incursion. Grant County prevailed."— *Blue Mountain Eagle*, Grant County's Newspaper

John Day Mayor Quinton commented on his community's response to the Aryan Nations: "That group keeps saying their values line up with ours and we're scratching our heads, trying to understand which values those are" (White supremacists eye property in John Day, 2010). The next morning after the events with the KCTFHR, *The Oregonian* newspaper in Portland quoted Stewart's opening remarks from the evening rally: "Tonight I declare victory for you. When you came together as one people with one voice and built a wall of unity, no hate can penetrate that wall" (T. Stewart, personal communication, August 19, 2019). He applauded the community's response, saying he had never seen such swift and complete community opposition to a threat from a hate group.

It was not long after that Jacob Green, an Aryan Nations Oregon state leader and Grant County resident, left the group saying "I have nothing to do with it—I'm withdrawing my participation" (I Quit' local man says, 2010). Green also stated that Cowan had left the group, too. Green said Mullet was an "old friend," however, he claimed he didn't speak up when Mullet announced his plan to create a national headquarters in John Day because Mullet was his "commander." He and Cowan had posed with Mullet for photographs at the newspaper following which he and his family received threats. He claimed that he did not want Mullet to relocate the headquarters; "I've been living almost 13 years here with no problem," he said. "I don't want to live next to that crap" (I Quit' local man says, 2010).

> ## POINTS TO PONDER
>
> Why did Jacob Green leave the group? How do you think the activism and organizing in John Day influenced this decision?

The final victory came when Paul Mullet announced he would not move to Grant County. After his visit to Grant County in February 2010, Paul Mullet relocated to Chillicothe, Ohio. He continued to claim his group was the real Aryan Nations (Callister, 2010b). His Aryan Nations website included information about the American National Socialist Party, with Mullet described as the "ANSP Reichsfuhrer." Contact information on the website directed people to a single e-mail address, "claiming that harassment and workplace threats have forced the 'pro-white' leaders to screen such contacts" with the same phone number used by Mullet when he was in John Day (Callister, 2010b). According to the group's teachings, only the White race is descended from Adam and Jews and non-Whites are natural enemies of White people. The mission, outlined on the group's website, is to create a state for the "Aryan race," separate from all non-Whites, and a "lawful Congress of our race." There is a 25-point call to action for all Whites to come together as a "Greater America," with citizenship only for those of pure White blood. The website also offered a tribute to Hitler's Waffen SS troops, copies of Hitler speeches, racist jokes and "cool slurs," and photos and articles about the late Richard Butler, founder of the Aryan Nations in Hayden, Idaho (White supremacists eye property in John Day, 2010).

HEADLINE

"A White supremacist leader who once set his sights on Grant County says he's settling in his former home state of Ohio, instead."—*Blue Mountain Eagle*, Neo-Nazi leader back in Ohio

POINTS TO PONDER

Why do you think Paul Mullet targeted this community as the town he wanted to relocate his headquarters into? How does this community response against the Aryan Nations challenge essentializing archetypal conceptions of rural communities? What do you think made John Day, Oregon—if anything—different from Chillicothe, Ohio?

THE WORK CONTINUES

The Maryland-based World Knights of the Ku Klux Klan became defunct in 2010 and members may have joined Mullet's group. Other activities that Mullet's group may have participated include a June demonstration in Pennsylvania at Gettysburg National Military Park and a July "White Unity Day" in Pulaski, Tennessee. The Southern Poverty Law Center (SPLC) reported that Mullet had sought donations to buy 15 acres of land in Tennessee for a new White homeland (Southern Poverty Law Center, Aryan Nations, n.d.).

POINTS TO PONDER

The fragmentation of a movement is something that has historically led to the fall of many social movements because it makes them ineffective. Do you think that the fragmentation of the White supremacist organization (seen through the fall and rise of various regional Klans, organizations, and leaders) makes it less or more effective at achieving its cause? Suppose it doesn't influence the White supremacist agenda, what makes White supremacist ideologies/movements more resilient than other sociopolitical movements?

Later in 2010, Mullet gave an interview to Ethos Magazine in which he remarked that with "2012 coming around the corner, that if something doesn't happen soon, that in this world, as we know it, there's going to be a pitched battle" (Southern Poverty Law Center, Paul Mullet, n.d.). Mullet became a part of the neo-Nazi group Crusaders for Yahweh-Aryan Nations LLC and took steps to become a Washington D.C. lobbyist. The Hill reported that Mullet said in his application that his group stands for "pro-white Christian identity [and] white nationalism" and will lobby on "any activities that adversely affect [sic] the White Race" (Wing, 2012).

DISCUSSION QUESTIONS

1.

Briefly describe the situation in the case. What aspects of your description are judgments (value statements about what is good or bad) and what aspects are objective statements?

2.

List multiple stakeholders in the case and identify the actions/strategies that each took. Why did each stakeholder (Paul Mullet, Scotta Callister, Tony Stewart, etc.) choose a particular strategy and what criteria did they use to determine what actions would be the "right" actions to take?

3.

What symbols, language, celebrations, stories, practices, and so on are used by each stakeholder to communicate what their group thinks is important and guides the behaviors of the group?

4.

How can rural communities ensure they have protections against encroachments from White supremacist organizations that may try to come into their community? What is the role of county and state governments to actively combat White supremacy? What is the role of media to actively counter White supremacy?

5.

What goal(s) can you envision for the outcomes in this case? Brainstorm new strategies for reaching the goal(s). What are the strengths and limitations of each?

6.

What lessons do you take away from this case and how might you apply them in your own context?

REFERENCES

Aney, K. (2018, April 20). *Tiny newspaper bucks a trend*. Retrieved March 2, 2020, from East Oregonian. https://www.eastoregonian.com/news/local/tiny-newspaper-bucks-a-trend/article_abb385ff-9653-543b-aca4-282e34a809e5.html

Associated Press. (2010, February 26). Ore. community comes together against supremacists. *The Spokesman-Review*. Retrieved March 2, 2020, from www.spokesman.com. https://www.spokesman.com/stories/2010/feb/26/ore-community-comes-together-against-supremacists/

Callister, S. (2010a, February 23). *Aryan Nations plan sparks protests in JD*. Retrieved from Blue Mountain Eagle. https://www.bluemountaineagle.com/news/aryan-nations-plan-sparks-protests-in-jd/article_a1c62cdf-06a4-53be-8428-890230788c7c.html

Callister, S. (2010b, December 28). *Mullet keeps busy—outside Grant County*. Retrieved March 2, 2020, from Blue Mountain Eagle. https://www.bluemountaineagle.com/news/mullet-keeps-busy-outside-grant-county/article_92f82a9c-26e2-5c38-9b3d-b54e3ea59eb4.html

Cariaga, D. (2010, February 19). *Sound and fury, signifying nothing: Aryan Nation poised to invade Oregon*. Retrieved March 2, 2020, from Sound and fury, signifying nothing. http://dadecariaga.blogspot.com/2010/02/aryan-nation-poised-to-invade-oregon.html

Cockle, R. (2010, February 27). *Grant county residents send message to white supremacists: Stay out*. Retrieved March 2, 2020, from oregonlive. https://www.oregonlive.com/news/2010/02/grant_county_residents_send_me.html

History. (n.d.). Retrieved from www.idahohumanrights.org. https://www.idahohumanrights.org/history.html

"I QUIT" local man says. (2010, February 23). Retrieved March 2, 2020, from Blue Mountain Eagle. https://www.bluemountaineagle.com/news/i-quit-local-man-says/article_42993a59-5769-5739-9cff-8720401138cb.html

Small Oregon town rallies against Aryan Nations. (2010, February 26). Retrieved March 2, 2020, from KHQ Right Now. https://www.khq.com/news/small-oregon-town-rallies-against-aryan-nations/article_f4b281b6-f0cb-5888-b8a0-d7a7ede6481c.html

Southern Poverty Law Center, Aryan Nations. (2010). Retrieved from Southern Poverty Law Center. https://www.splcenter.org/fighting-hate/extremist-files/group/aryan-nations

Southern Poverty Law Centre, Paul Mullet. (n.d.). Retrieved March 2, 2020, from Southern Poverty Law Center. https://www.splcenter.org/fighting-hate/extremist-files/individual/paul-mullet

Stewart, T., & Gissel, N. (2012). Choosing social justice over hate: Two stories of community success in the Pacific Northwest. *National Civic Review*, 101(2), 38–43. https://doi.org/10.1002/ncr.21075

White supremacists eye property in John Day. (2010, February 18). Retrieved March 2, 2020, from The Astorian. https://www.dailyastorian.com/news/white-supremacists-eye-property-in-john-day/article_0349c109-84e0-5643-8e0e-a9d95b6a904a.html

Wing, N. (2012, June 18). *White nationalist Neo-Nazi birther heads to the hill.* Retrieved March 2, 2020, from HuffPost. https://www.huffpost.com/entry/paul-mullet-white-nationalist-neo-nazi-lobbyist_n_1607179

THE STORY IN NORTH DAKOTA

OVERVIEW

Usama Dakdok, founder of the Straight Way of Grace Ministry, held a rally on March 17, 2015 at the Empire Center in Grand Forks, North Dakota. At the rally, 200 people were in the audience to hear Dakdok's messages that included "Allah is Satan" and that Islam was a "cult and disease." Dakdok made plans to return to Grand Forks in September of that year (Forum News Service, 2015). With the leadership of Debbie Storrs, University of North Dakota (UND) Dean of the College of Arts and Sciences, the community was divided about what to do. Should the owners of the Empire Arts Center where Dakdok was to speak cancel the event? Some people opposed Dakdok's message but defended his right of "Free Speech." Others wanted to organize a nonviolent protest outside the venue, while others considered organizing an alternative gathering at a different site. Should the community choose one or more of these strategies? What other strategies could they consider?

Timeline

2001	The Straight Way of Grace Founded by Usama Dakdok
2015	Dakdok Invited to Speak in North Dakota
2015, March	People Protested Against Dakdok's Message
2015, April	"Meet Your Muslim Neighbor" Event
2015, September	Dakdok Planed Another Event in Grand Forks; The Dean of Social Arts and Sciences Reached Out to the Kootenai County Task Force on Human Relations (KCTFHR); Local Leaders, Along With the University of North Dakota, North Dakotans for Diversity and Compassion, and the KCTFHR held a Diversity and Inclusion Event
2015, November	Dakdok Spoke for a Third Time in Grand Forks (Invited by Council Member Terry Bjerke)
2015, December	Molotov Cocktail Thrown into a Somali-Owned Restaurant
2016	Federal Bureau of Investigation (FBI) Records Indicated Two Hate Crimes in Grand Forks and Eight Overall Within the State

BACKGROUND: UNIVERSITY OF NORTH DAKOTA AND GRAND FORKS ENCOUNTERS WITH THE STRAIGHT WAY OF GRACE MINISTRY

The UND, the state's oldest and largest university, has about 15,000 students (About UND, n.d.). Grand Forks County is in the easternmost region of the state, in the Red River Valley, which covers the eastern strip bordering Minnesota. This region is proud of its rich farmland, producing wheat, corn, soybeans, sugar beets, and potatoes (Pates, 2020).

Usama Dakdok had no connection to North Dakota until he was invited to speak by Phil Ehlke, the general manager of the Christian radio station Q-FM in 2015. Dakdok was born in Egypt and raised in a Christian home (The Straight Way of Grace Ministry, About Us, n.d.). While attending school in Egypt, Dakdok was taught about Islam and later studied Sharia Law during his time at university. At some point, Dakdok joined the Covenant Players, a professional theatre company that shared the message of Jesus Christ through

© Ken Wolter/Shutterstock.com

a performance. While serving in the Covenant Players in England, he met his future wife, Vicki, whom he married in 1991. Eventually in 1992, Dakdok and his wife moved to the United States where they settled in Florida. In 1997, Dakdok and his wife welcomed their only child, a son, named Caleb. Dakdok holds a Bachelor's Degree in Theology and a Master's Degree in Missiology from New Orleans Baptist Theological Seminary.

Upon his arrival in the United States, Dakdok believed that with his depth of knowledge in Islam, he could reach out to the Muslims in America and share the Gospel of Jesus Christ (The Straight Way of Grace Ministry, About Us, n.d.). This was at least in part the motivation for founding The Straight Way of Grace Ministry in 2001. Additionally, Dakdok, whose native language is Arabic, believed that the English translation of the Qur'an was "full of misrepresentations that minimized its violent teaching as written in the Arabic text" (The Straight Way of Grace Ministry, About Us, n.d., para. 6). Dakdok's first project was a book titled, The Generous Qur'an, which according to him "is an accurate English translation [of the Qur'an] with study notes and material to help Christians share the Gospel with Muslims" (The Straight Way of Grace Ministry, About Us, n.d., para. 6). Dakdok continued his criticism of Islam in his second book, Exposing the Truth about the Qur'an, The Revelation of Error. Exposing the Truth about the Qur'an according to Dakdok "discuss[es] the many hundreds of geographical, historical, moral, theological, legal, scientific, and linguistic errors contained in Islam's holiest book" (Usama Dakdok Publishing, LLC, 2010, para. 2). Both of Dakdok's books were met with criticism by many Muslims who believed that he was unqualified to translate the Qur'an and his translation was incorrect and/or taken out of context (Snow, 2013).

The Straight Way of Grace Ministry's doctrine states, "we have been charged to address 'certain needs' of our own generation. In an age increasingly hostile to Christian truth, our challenge is to express the truth as revealed in Scripture, and to bear witness to Jesus Christ, who is 'the Way, the Truth, and the Life'" (The Straight Way of Grace Ministry, Our Doctrinal Statement, n.d., para. 17). The Straight Way of Grace Ministry website provides multiple resources to Muslims to help Muslims learn about Jesus Christ (The Straight Way of Grace Ministry, n.d.). The website also encourages not only Christians, but every American, to learn about Islam, through various resources on their website including radio shows, books, DVDs, newsletters, and teaching articles. In addition to the online resources, Dakdok, along with his Ministry, travels across the county discussing his understanding of Islam.

2015: "MEET YOUR NEIGHBOR"

In 2015, Dakdok was invited to speak in North Dakota by Phil Ehlke, the general manager of the Christian radio station Q-FM. According to Ehlke, the purpose of this event was to "instruct people about what Islam is" (Richie, 2015a, para. 3). Dakdok believed through his events he was educating his attendees.

Upon hearing of Dakdok's scheduled event, various organizations, including members of the UND's Muslim Student Association, the Christus Rex Lutheran Campus Ministry, North Dakotans Against Brutality, Free Thinkers of UND, B'Nai Israel Synagogue, Third Wave Feminist Group UND, the North Dakota Human Rights Coalition, Council on American-Islamic Relations—Minnesota, and the Grand Forks Islamic Center formed the North Dakotans for Interfaith Acceptance over a weekend (Richie, 2015a). The North Dakotans for Interfaith Acceptance organized a counter-protest to Dakdok's event and applied and received the appropriate permits from the Grand Forks Police Department (Richie, 2015a).

On March 17, the counter-protestors marched toward the location of Dakdok's event at the Empire Event Center and stood silently outside until the end of Dakdok's event. The group was instructed to remain silent during the counter-protest to ensure that there was no escalation to violence (Richie, 2015a). When anyone attempted to interact or speak with the counter-protestors, the counter-protestors simply handed out a card that identified their intentions of silently counter-protesting (Richie, 2015a).

Dakdok's event, which drew approximately 200 attendees, was titled "Revealing the Jihad and Terrorism of Islam." The presentation addressed multiple facets of Islam, including topics of world domination, doctrines, laws, and infiltration into America (The Straight Way of Grace, Presentations, n.d.). Dakdok used short passages from both the Bible

© Ink Drop/Shutterstock.com

and the Qur'an, put next to each other, and drew his conclusions. One of his most prominent conclusions was "Allah is Satan." According to an article written by Dakdok and found on the Allah is Satan page of The Straight Way of Grace Ministry website (n.d.), he identifies verses from the Qur'an 1:1 and 2 Corinthians 4:4, and comparing "Allah is the god (lord) of this world: The praise be to Allah, the lord of the worlds" to "the god of this world is Satan" (para. 3). Based upon these two texts, Dakdok concluded that Allah is Satan.

POINTS TO PONDER

Are there different interpretations of Allah? Do we know what Arabic speaking Christians call God? Imagine that you are a practicing Muslim in North Dakota, how might you feel hearing that an invited speaker says that "Allah is Satan"? Does this statement fall under free speech? What evidence can you provide for your position?

In addition to organizing the march and silent protest, the North Dakotans for Interfaith Acceptance planned an alternative event, "Meet Your Muslim Neighbor." The "Meet Your Muslim Neighbor" event occurred on April 7, 2015 and was attended by nearly 200 people (Jacobs & Herald, 2015, p. 1). The purpose of the event was to break bread and learn about Islam through dialogue. The event included a panel of Muslims who answered questions from audience members. The questions ranged from what Islam says about women to how Islam views Jesus and if Islam condones violence (Richie, 2015a). The panel members were quick to refute Dakdok's idea that Islam is a terrorist religion. In fact, panel members stated that anyone could interpret a verse of the Qur'an out of context to justify their actions. According to Mehdi Ostadhassan, an associate professor of engineering at the UND and faculty advisor for the Muslim Student Association, "specific verses in the Quran referred to specific situations in the past, and how radical groups such as ISIS have taken such verses out of context to accomplish their own ends" (Richie, 2015b, para. 16). Additionally, Nabil Suleiman, president of the Grand Forks Islamic Center and an associate professor in the UND College of Engineering and Mines, stated that "any commands to go to war referred to the Muslim army of Quranic times fighting back in a specific way to not be eliminated, but the instructions also prohibited killing women or children or destroying or burning property" (Richie, 2015b, para. 17). Ultimately, the panel discussion refuted Dakdok's statements that Islam was a terrorist religion and that those who wish to cause harm, can easily misinterpret Qur'an or Biblical verses to justify and accomplish their own means.

POINTS TO PONDER

On what basis does Dakdok claim to be an expert on Islam? To what extent do we value Islamic knowledge from practicing Muslims? From someone educated about Islam, but not a practicing Muslim? How would you have responded to Dakdok's messages of Islam in your community? Do you think events like the silent protest or the "Meet Your Muslim Neighbor" were effective in mitigating the narrative being promoted by Dakdok in the community?

The "Meet Your Muslim Neighbor" event ended with Muslim's participating in one of Islam's five daily prayers and those gathered at the event were invited to observe the daily prayer. Finally, food from various cultures was provided to all those in attendance.

2015: MENTORING FROM THE KOOTENAI COUNTY TASK FORCE ON HUMAN RELATIONS

Dakdok made plans to return to Grand Forks in September of 2015. Dakdok received a DVD of the April "Meet Your Muslim Neighbor" event (Jacobs, 2015) and during his September speech, he compared the April event to his English translation of the Qur'an. Ultimately, Dakdok concluded that the April event was a recruiting effort to convert individuals to Islam.

The community was split on how to respond to Dakdok's second appearance in Grand Forks. There were individuals who wanted to vocally protest Dakdok's speech, there were some who wanted the venue to cancel the event, and still others who wanted to organize a peaceful, alternative gathering. Debbie Storrs, UND Dean of the College of Arts and Sciences, reached out to Tony Stewart and Norm Gissel of the Kootenai County Task Force on Human Relations in an attempt to bridge the various responses into one united front.

Ultimately, in response to Dakdok's second event, local leaders, in partnership with the UND and the North Dakotans for Diversity and Compassion (NDDC) provided an alternative fellowship opportunity that included food and discussion. The goal of this counter event was to come together as a community and discuss diversity and inclusion. This event, held at St. Paul's Episcopal Church, was held the same evening of Dakdok's speech. This counter event featured Stewart and Gissel from the Kootenai County Task Force on Human Relations, who discussed strategies for community inclusiveness and compassion. There was no counter demonstration outside of the Empire Event Center of Dakdok's speech.

In addition to speaking during the evening, both Stewart and Gissel spent the morning visiting with classes on the campus of the UND. Throughout the day, and particularly at the alternative gathering, Stewart and Gissel emphasized nonviolence while celebrating diversity. Stewart said, "Community members should always speak out against hate speech, but they should never attend meetings of any discriminatory group, and they should never engage in violence. Be in charge of your culture and watch and look, and anytime someone goes through [discrimination], become their ally. So many people suffer because of what they've been through, and they don't have any ally, and they need one" (Haley, 2015, para. 26). Stewart and Gissel met with several University of North Dakota (UND) clubs and community groups during their three day visit.

POINTS TO PONDER

Is there a positive reason to attend a gathering of a discriminatory group? Is attending a meeting of a discriminatory group to gather information and be better informed a good reason to attend? Is safety a concern? If community members do not attend these types of meetings, is the responsibility left to groups such as the FBI? Are there times in history when information gathered by the FBI was biased or wrong? If yes, what then?

Stewart and Gissel also attended an informal meeting with local city leaders, the day after Dakdok's second speech. This informal meeting, requested by City Council member Bret Weber, was intended to "consider efforts to clearly express that this (Grand Forks) is an inclusive and welcoming community" (Haley, 2015, para. 2). Additionally, this meeting provided an opportunity to discuss the balance of a citizen's right to free speech and the community's responsibility to protect residents from discrimination (Haley, 2015).

POINTS TO PONDER

Is it necessarily true that closing meetings to the media means that attendees will feel more comfortable speaking freely? What are the strengths and limitations to meetings closed to the media? To meetings open to the media?

2015: DAKOTANS FOR DIVERSITY AND COMPASSION AND THE GLOBAL FRIENDS COALITION

The speeches by Usama Dakdok as well as the community's reactions highlighted tensions that had been previously hidden in Grand Forks. Community members began to debate whether or not Dakdok's rhetoric was protected free speech or should be banned from the community, and while the community took some immediate actions to bond together, the sense of cohesion did not hold. The speeches by Dakdok brought both community anti-hate bonding and emboldened hate supporters.

Dakdok continued his anti-Islam efforts. He continued to tour around the U.S. making speeches and in November 2015, Dakdok returned to Grand Forks for the third time in eight months. City council member Terry Bjerke invited Dakdok to return on the grounds that the protests against Dakdok's prior speeches violated 1st Amendment rights. "Our country is founded on free speech, political and religious free speech is one of the founding blocks of this country and so I think it's important that whenever there's an attempt to silence political and religious speech that as citizens we speak up and defend it," said Terry Bjerke, Grand Forks City Council Ward 1 (T. Stewart, personal communication, August 19, 2019). Bjerke not only sent the invitation, he donated part of his council salary for it and spoke with Dakdok on stage. Phil Elke, Q-FM Radio General Manager once again sponsored the event, calling it the "Celebrate Freedom Event" (McMahon, 2015).

> ## HEADLINE
>
> Bjerke, Dakdok team up for freedom of speech event | Grand Forks Herald

The Community flared with tensions. People spoke out against the anti-Islam rhetoric of Dakdok, including writing op-eds both in local newspapers and national blogs (Khan, 2015). This perpetuated the conversation on where the line of free speech should be drawn. Some community members found Dakdok's words offensive, but still maintained them to be free speech. Councilman Bjerke's stand for free speech drew criticism from fellow community leaders. During this November event, Bjerke delivered a 20-minute speech to a nearly packed

theater ahead of Dakdok's speech, passionately defending the free speech rights of Dakdok and handing out copies of the Declaration of Independence and the Constitution (Easter, 2017).

The continued community tensions boiled over soon after Dakdok's third appearance. Grand Forks began to see an uptick in anti-Islam activity in the community in late 2015. On December 8, 2015, a man threw a Molotov cocktail through the front window of Juba Coffee House and Restaurant, a Somali-owned restaurant which also served as a cultural hub for Somali residents. The attacker was sentenced to 15 years in prison (Report, 2016). Despite the defendant refusing to talk about the event, the community believed the actions were racially motivated and that the man was also responsible for spray painting a Nazi symbol and the words "Go Home" on the restaurant just days before the Molotov cocktail incident (Carlson, 2015b). While the defendant repeatedly refused to confirm his motivations, the incident occurred just hours after Donald Trump, a U.S. presidential front-runner, called for a ban on Muslims entering the country (Samuels, 2015).

HEADLINE

Global Friends to step up efforts to help integrate refugees into Grand Forks | Grand Forks Herald

There were no injuries from the fire caused by the Molotov cocktail, but fire caused an estimated $90,000 in damage. Both the local community and sympathizers across America reacted to assist the ailing business. Former UND professor Coleen Berry, living in Colorado, set up a GoFundMe page, which raised over $20,000 to support the recovery. Locally, several organizations such as Hope Church, NDDC, the Global Friends Coalition, in addition to local artists, musicians, and community members, offered assistance (T. Stewart, personal communication, August 19, 2019). The Global Friends Coalition, a nonprofit which helps refugees settle into the area, cited the arson at the Somali restaurant as a reason for increased donations which allowed them to expand their operations (Johnson, 2016). Local fundraising events featuring art and music were held to generate money to help rebuild (Bjorke, Bonham, & Johnson, 2015). After the arson, Dakdok spoke to a local news station and unabashedly continued his anti-Islam rhetoric stating that "I believe Satan will use Islam to bring destruction to all planet earth, as you will see it coming in the next few years" (Carlson, 2015a).

In the months after Dakdok's last speech and the arson, community members attempted to form a diversity commission to advise the city council, and held a public forum. The proponents cited the speeches by Dakdok as the impetus of the idea and stated that the city felt more united following Dakdok's speeches than before. Sixty percent of people who spoke at the city council's forum fully supported the diversity commission (Rupard, 2015). However, support for the idea waned as the public memory of the speeches faded. Activists who drove the discussion left the area, and while there was pervading public recognition of the need to counter hate, especially anti-immigrant hate, no leaders emerged to push the idea into fruition, and at the time of this case, no diversity commission has been formed in Grand Forks (Easter, 2017).

POINTS TO PONDER

What is your understanding of the distinction between free speech and hate speech? What strategies help a community balance the benefits of outside expertise with the need for local leadership? What is at risk if this balance is not carefully considered?

THE WORK CONTINUES

According to Federal Bureau of Investigation (FBI) records, in 2016 North Dakota recorded eight hate crimes, seven for racial bias and one for religious discrimination. North Dakota ranked second in the country for hate crimes by population in 2014 and 2015, but dropped to 38th among the states and the District of Columbia, owed in part to the denominator effect of the population increase due to the oil boom. Two of the eight incidents in 2016 occurred in Grand Forks, including an anti-African American incident on UND, and an anti-Islam incident in the city of Grand Forks. In the latter incident, a Muslim airman stationed at Grand Forks Air Force Base was harassed and assaulted in downtown Grand Forks by a man who called him a "terrorist," "Osama Bin Laden," and "Saddam Hussein," and told him to "get out of my country" (Hazzard, 2017).

Usama Dakdok continued to live in Florida, his state of residence since 1992, and continued to publish anti-Islam material through his speaking tours, his website, and his books.

DISCUSSION QUESTIONS

1.

Briefly describe the situation in the case. What aspects of your description are judgments (value statements about what is good or bad) and what aspects are objective statements?

2.

Should hate speech be protected under the freedom of speech outlined in the Constitution? Why or why not?

3.

What are some effective strategies the case study illustrated that did not violate anyone's freedom of speech while still promoting diversity and inclusion? Were these efforts effective? Why or why not?

4.

What goal(s) can you envision for the outcomes in this case? Brainstorm new strategies for reaching the goal(s). What are the strengths and limitations of each?

5.

What lessons do you take away from this case and how might you apply them in your own context?

REFERENCES

About UND. (n.d.). Retrieved from https://und.edu/about/index.html

About Us: Covenant Players. (n.d.). Retrieved from http://covenantplayers.org/about-us/

Bjorke, C., Bonham, K., & Johnson, J. (2015, December 7). Arson at grand forks Somali restaurant followed swastika graffiti. *Pioneer Press*. Retrieved from https://www.twincities.com/2015/12/07/arson-at-grand-forks-somali-restaurant-followed-swastika-graffiti/

Carlson, N. (2015a, December 17). *Grand forks leader calls Islam peaceful, Dakdok says it means world domination*. Retrieved from http://www.valleynewslive.com/home/headlines/GF-leader-calls-Islam-peaceful-Dakdok-says-it-means-world-domination-362834461.html

Carlson, N. (2015b, December 18). *Suspect in grand forks juba coffee shop arson fire clams up*. Retrieved from http://www.valleynewslive.com/home/headlines/Suspect-in-Grand-Forks-Juba-Coffee-Shop-arson-fire-clams-up-362968011.html

Easter, S. (2017, October 1). *Does grand forks still need a diversity commission?* Retrieved from http://www.grandforksherald.com/news/4336267-does-grand-forks-still-need-diversity-commission

Forum Service News. (2015, March 17). *Anti-Islam Christian speaker Usama Dakdok draws protests, crowds in GF; to speak in Bagley Wednesday night*. Retrieved from Bemidji Pioneer. https://www.bemidjipioneer.cm/news/3702657-anti-islam-christian-speaker-usama-dakdok-draws-protests-crowds-gf-speak-bagley

Haley, C. (2015, September 4). Local leaders to hold meeting in response to anti-Islam event. *Grand Forks Herald*. Retrieved from: www.nexisuni.com

Hazzard, A. (2017, November 24). *Two grand forks incidents recorded in FBI hate crimes report*. Retrieved from http://www.grandforksherald.com/news/4364116-two-grand-forks-incidents-recorded-fbi-hate-crimes-report

Jacobs, B. (2015, September 4). Dakdok refutes 'Meet your Muslim neighbor.' *Grand Forks Herald*. Retrieved from https://issuu.com/molsteadlibraryatnic/docs/kootenai_county_task_force_on_human

Jacobs, B., & Herald, F. G. (2015, September 3). *Watch now: Dakdok back for rebuttal, protesters not*. Retrieved February 28, 2020, from Grand Forks Herald.

https://www.grandforksherald.com/news/3831891-watch-now-dakdok-back-rebuttal-protesters-not

Johnson, J. (2016, January 2). *Global friends to step up efforts to help integrate refugees*. Retrieved from http://www.grandforksherald.com/news/3915813-global-friends-step-efforts-help-integrate-refugees-grand-forks

Khan, A. (2015, May 7). *Fighting arguments with arguments, not violence*. Retrieved from https://www.huffingtonpost.com/ahmed-khan/fighting-arguments-with-a_b_7229278.html

McMahon, K. (2015, October 7). *Usama dakdok returns to grand forks*. Retrieved from http://www.wdaz.com/news/3856304-usama-dakdok-returns-grand-forks

Our Doctrinal Statement: The Straight Way. (n.d.). Retrieved from http://www.thestraightway.org/our-doctrinal-statement/

Pates, M. (2020, January 13). *Tech helps beet farmers strategize for spring*. Retrieved February 28, 2020, from Agweek. https://www.agweek.com/business/agriculture/4699542-tech-helps-beet-farmers-strategize-spring

Presentations: The Straight Way. (n.d.). Retrieved from http://www.thestraightway.org/presentations/

Report, H. S. (2016, September 6). *Arsonist receives 15 years for blaze set at Somali restauran*. Retrieved from http://www.grandforksherald.com/news/4109388-arsonist-receives-15-years-blaze-set-somali-restaurant

Richie, G. (2015a, April 8). Panel, discussion night encourages interfaith dialogue and acceptance. *Grand Forks Herald*. Retrieved from www.nexisuni.com

Richie, G. (2015b, March 18). Crowds come to protest, attend speech by Christian speaker Usama Dakdok. *Grand Forks Herald*. Retrieved from www.nexisuni.com

Rupard, W. (2015, November 3). *Bjerke, Dakdok team up for freedom of speech event*. Retrieved from http://www.grandforksherald.com/news/3874484-bjerke-dakdok-team-freedom-speech-event

Samuels, R. (2015, December 29). Trump's effect on Muslim migrant debate reverberates in heartland. *Washington Post*. Retrieved from https://www.washingtonpost.com/politics/trumps-effect-on-muslim-migrant-debate-reverberates-in-heartland/2015/12/29/0fd05b4a-a818-11e5-bff5-905b92f5f94b_story.html

Snow, Y. (2013, April 27). *The facts about Islam: Usama dakdok is similar to ergun caner* [correcting usama dakdok on his 'the 'the generous quran' quran' title]. Retrieved from http://thefactsaboutislam.blogspot.com/2013/04/usama-dakdoks-ignorance-on-front-page.html

The Straight Way. (n.d.). Retrieved from http://www.thestraightway.org

Usama Dakdok Publishing, LLC. (2010). Retrieved from http://www.usamapublishing.com/

Chapter 11

CASE STUDY: THE STORY IN WASHINGTON

© Olinchuk/Shutterstock.com

OVERVIEW

In 1992, public officials and business leaders in Stevens County, Washington became deeply concerned after a White supremacist pastor's visit to Colville for the purpose of distributing anti-Semitic literature, followed by Aryan Nations' member Justin Dwyer and skinhead recruit Elizabeth Bullis moving to the county (Kitsap Sun, 1992). In response, a public meeting was scheduled where leaders of the Kootenai County Task Force on Human Relations (KCTFHR) were invited to speak. Hundreds of local citizens attended the standing-room-only event. The meeting was so well-attended that extra chairs were placed in the aisle, lined the walls, and clogged the foyer with the crowd spilling into the parking lot. As the president of the KCTFHR Tony Stewart told the audience: "Supremacists attempt to disguise themselves at the beginning but it doesn't take long until you will learn from their talk and actions their true intent" (T. Stewart, personal communication, August 19, 2019). This public meeting led to the formation of the Upper Columbia Human Rights Coalition that functioned for several years. After a rather long period of inaction and the rise of new challenges in Stevens County, the original group invited journalist Bill Morlin, attorney Norm Gissel, and Tony Stewart back to the community on November 18, 2016 to help reorganize the Upper Columbia Human Rights Coalition that is now active again.

Timeline

1991, July	Skinhead Recruiting Trip Along the West Coast of Oregon and Washington
1991, December	Neo-Nazi Rally Honoring Robert (Bob) Mathews of The Order
1992, June 4	KCTFHR Travels to Colville Community
1992	Aryan Nations Leader Departs Based on Eugenics Doctrine
1998, 2009	"Hands Across the Border for Human Rights" Parts I and II
2010, 2018	Westboro Baptist Church (WBC) Pickets
2016	Upper Columbia Human Rights Coalition Reinvigorated
2019	Spokane Youth Minister and Youth Group Attacked in Coeur d'Alene

BACKGROUND: KING COUNTY AND STEVENS COUNTY, WASHINGTON ARE INTRODUCED TO "RACIALNOMICS"

Washington ranks 18th in the United States in terms of geographic size, with the Cascade Mountains creating a clear line of distinction between the west side and the east side, the temperate and the arid climates, and the blue and the red voters of the state (Washington, n.d.). Snohomish, King and Pierce counties of the state accounted for more than half of the state's approximate population of seven million in 2019 (Washington Population 2019 [Demographics, Maps, Graphs], 2019). The east side of the state begins with the Cascade Mountains moving eastwards to the Idaho border (Cascade Range Mountains, United States, 2020). The vast majority of eastern Washington has a population density of zero to 50 people per square mile (Office of Financial Management, n.d.). Stevens County, bordered by Canada on the north, is in the northeast corner of Washington and is situated near the Washington–Idaho state border. It has a population density of zero to 20 people per square mile (Office of Financial Management, n.d.). Overall, the state is rich in agricultural production (apples, dairy, cattle, and potatoes) and industry (lumber, tourism, hydroelectric power, computer software, aircraft, and aluminum refining) and has had a steady growth in population since the beginning of the 20th century. The state is a part of what was formerly known as the Oregon Territory and the portion east of the Cascade Mountains is commonly referred to as part of the Inland Northwest (About Washington, n.d.).

Floyd Cochran also saw the beauty of Washington and the Inland Northwest; however, he came for the Aryan Nations in neighboring Hayden, Idaho. Cochran had spent his childhood in upstate New York, but was down and out when he moved to the Aryan Nations compound and became a top officer. He became the face of the Aryan Nations, providing public relations with a nonthreatening effective message for recruiting (Up From Hatred, 1997). As the leading spokesperson, he wore a blue uniform with fascist shoulder patches but no guns when he gave press conferences. Even with his less menacing approach, he was committed to hate. He embraced the Aryan Nations' mantras that Jews were "Satan's offspring," Blacks were "animals," and homosexuals were "evil perverts" (Up From Hatred, 1997). By acknowledging these hateful beliefs and being White, he could belong to what he considered to be a master race and gain a sense of courage and importance. "It made people notice me, and not just for a day or two. It really made an impression. I enjoyed that" (Up From Hatred, 1997).

Aryan Nations doctrine claims that White people are the "chosen people" of God and Cochran worked for Richard Butler's vision to prepare for war for the purpose of creating a Whites-only homeland in five Northwest states (Ostendorf, 2002). For his first major assignment, Cochran brought a group of young skinheads to a public ceremony in Idaho that was honoring Dr. Martin Luther King Jr. Cochran and the group of skinheads walked into the church and stood. With just their presence, they were able to disrupt the choir, and feel a sense of their own power and ability to spread fear (Up From Hatred, 1997).

In his talks, Cochran addressed people who were unemployed or afraid about their economic future, and he got attention on mainstream media. He would connect to his audience, moving from hate of the state, to hate of a people, and then protection of their own (White) race. One of Cochran's communication pieces showed Seattle sex workers with music from the Guns 'n' Roses' song "Welcome to the Jungle" playing. The scene in the video turned to a park with Aryan Nations' mothers wheeling baby strollers and closed with the Aryan Nations' address (T. Stewart, personal communication, August 19, 2019).

In July 1991, Cochran and a group of skinheads planned a recruiting trip along the west coast of Oregon and Washington, visiting timber towns. Justin Dwyer had been a skinhead in the San Francisco Bay area before coming to the Aryan Nations in the late 1980s and becoming the chief Aryan Nations organizer for the state of Washington. Cochran and Dwyer's message was one of networking and "racialnomics," saying "Our message is, we're here to protect you and your family, and we can do it better than a multiracial government." (Richard, 1991). Community members asked Robert Hughes, a member of the U.S. Justice Department's Community Relations Service and Board member of the Northwest Coalition Against Malicious Harassment, to speak about the Aryan Nations. In a meeting with approximately 100 people in attendance, Hughes told the audience that the Aryan Nations' message would be less overt White supremacy and instead focus on (White) workers' economic insecurities (Richard, 1991). Following the meeting, the community issued an anti-hate statement, warning hate groups to stay away and saying that the hate groups were not welcome.

> ## POINTS TO PONDER
>
> White supremacists use economic issues/concerns as an area of focus to gain traction. Why is this choice strategic for these groups to recruit members? Are people drawn into supremacist groups because they are hateful, or because they are financially desperate? What makes a person more or less susceptible to White supremacist ideologies?

In September 1991, Dwyer sponsored 25 Aryan youth and skinheads at Salt Water State Park in south King County. In October 1991, he used racist fliers for recruiting, disseminating the message that "members of the Aryan Nations share the belief that the 'white race' is more highly evolved than other races and purporting that people who are not white were created as a work force for the planet" (ADL, 2017). Maintaining the flow of activities, in December 1991, Dwyer honored the late Robert (Bob) Mathews, who had founded the violent splinter group "The Order", with a neo-Nazi rally.

In 1992, Dwyer left his home, wife, and two children in northwest Washington and moved to Stevens County in the northeast corner of the state with skinhead recruit Elizabeth Bullis. Skinheads had been recruited to revitalize the aging membership of Aryan Nations. Dwyer wasn't getting a divorce because "we don't believe in courts or anything like that, only God's law" (Kitsap Sun, 1992). John Sheppard took the Aryan Nations' leadership role for western Washington. The White supremacy youth leaders (Dwyer was 24 years old and Bullis was 21) promised to continue their involvement. Dwyer stayed out of the headlines. He was awarded a concealed weapon permit soon after moving to Stevens County.

Civil rights leaders expected increased racist activity with the move of Dwyer and Bullis to eastern Washington. Bill Wassmuth, director of the Northwest Coalition Against Malicious Harassment, said there had been an increase in Aryan Nations fliers in Pullman, Spokane, and near Newport, Washington (Kitsap Sun, 1992).

> ## HEADLINE
>
> "Good people must act."—*Spokesman-Review* Editorial, Tuesday May 12, 1992. Kootenai County Task Force on Human Relations Scrapbooks 1992 by Molstead Library at North Idaho College

Elizabeth Bullis, the daughter of a wealthy San Francisco family, was one of the first female racist skinhead leaders to break the neo-Nazi gender barrier.She became the "National Secretary" of the American Front, an organization that called for a "Third Position: Revolutionary Racial Nationalism" (Crawford, Garder, Mozzochi, & Taylor, 1994). The American Front was generally distrusted by groups aligned with Hitler's version of Nazism (including the Aryan Nations), because of their potential political left leanings. The Third Position called for an environmentalist alternative to "consumer capitalism" and "industrial communism" by blending animal rights and (White) women's rights with racist, anti-Semitic, and homophobic positions. The American Front also disavowed immigrant labor at the expense of the White working class and attacked right leaning corporations for destroying the environment in pursuit of profits. The group recruited through night time literature drops, putting fliers on vehicle windshields and doorsteps with contact information (Crawford et al., 1994).

1990s: THE BIRTH OF THE UPPER COLUMBIA HUMAN RIGHTS COALITION

Working with the Colville Chamber of Commerce, Stevens County commissioners scheduled a public meeting to get advice from Kootenai County Task Force on Human Relations (KCTFHR) members Tony Stewart, Jeanne Givens, and Marshall Mend at an evening program held on June 4, 1992. Hundreds of local citizens attended the event at the Fort Colville Grange Hall with extra chairs in the aisle, lining the walls, and clogging the foyer. The crowd spilled into the parking lot. The KCTFHR showed one of their documentaries and spoke to those present. Tony Stewart, president of the KCTFHR, told the audience: "Supremacists attempt to disguise themselves at the beginning but it doesn't take long until you will learn from their talk and actions of their true intent" (T. Stewart, personal communication, August 19, 2019). The meeting was held to take a stand against Dwyer. The outcome of the rally was the establishment of the Upper Columbia Human Rights Coalition in Stevens County, Washington.

Richard Butler had started holding events to recruit youth into the Aryan Nations, organizing an annual April gathering to celebrate Hitler's birthday, which came to be known as the Aryan Nations or Hitler Youth Festival (Meagan, 2017). Around the time of the 1992 gathering, Dwyer left the Aryan Nations claiming differences over policies involving youth and women. Others also left the Aryan Nations, including Washington state security chief Brad Williams and Western Washington leader John Sheppard (Associated Press, 1992). Leaders from Montana and southern Tennessee also left possibly over differences with the identified future Aryan Nations leader Carl Franklin (Southern Poverty Law Center, Aryan Nations, n.d.). With many rumors about the departures, the attendance at the Aryan Nations World Conference in July was smaller and only about 150 were at the cross burning.

Franklin suggested that it was the pressure from human rights activists in Colville that was a reason for Dwyer's resignation from the Aryan Nations. Floyd Cochran remained committed to the Aryan Nations cause, saying "Naturally we are not going to roll up the carpet and go home. We'll handle things from here" (Associated Press, 1992). But then a man at the Aryan Nations compound began talking about the commitment to eugenics with Cochran. Cochran had a son with a cleft palate and following the eugenics doctrine would mean that all people with a genetic abnormality (a disability or deformity) would be euthanized in the Aryan Promised Land—including his son. It wasn't long until Cochran also left the Aryan Nations (and White supremacy all together).

Upon Floyd Cochran's departure from the Aryan Nations, he called KCTFHR's Tony Stewart. The two held an hour long conversation during which Cochran shared his involvement with the Aryan Nations and his desire to change his life around to be an advocate for human rights. Stewart advised Cochran he could become a powerful force for good.

Dwyer may have maintained his relationship with Richard Butler given that in April 1994, the Aryan Nations founder presided over Dwyer's marriage ceremony that was held beneath a burning swastika during an Aryan Youth Conference (Morlin, 1996).

In 1995, Dwyer became a seasonal federal law officer, working six months a year for the National Park Service at Fort Spokane, in the southern tip of Stevens County. Dwyer, aged 28, told the *Spokesman-Review* newspaper that he was no longer involved with the Aryan Nations. "I'm trying to put the past behind me and (a news story) will only be counterproductive in my new life," Dwyer said. "I am no longer involved (in Aryan Nations) and haven't been for several years." Noting that employers are prohibited from asking job applicants about membership in unions and political or religious organizations, the superintendent of the Coulee Dam National Recreation Area said "If we'd known then what we know now about him, the National Park Service would have never hired this guy" (Morlin, 1996).

POINTS TO PONDER

Should employers be able to ask applicants if they are associated/affiliated with supremacy organizations? What would the implications of that be for religious/political discrimination and rights to privacy?

In 1999, Dwyer moved to Prescott, Arizona. He got a job as a detention officer and was promoted to deputy in 2000. Although he denounces White supremacy, he struggled in his personal life. In September 2008, Dwyer, aged 41, pleaded guilty to providing drugs and alcohol (marijuana and cocaine) to minors at homemade pornography viewing parties. He was sentenced to seven and a half years in prison, with no chance for parole.

1998: "HANDS ACROSS THE BORDER FOR HUMAN RIGHTS": PARTS I AND II

In January 1998, the KCTFHR Board became aware that not only would the Aryan Nations hold their annual Aryan Nations World Congress in July at the compound on Rimrock above Hayden, Idaho, but also that the Aryan Nations would march on the main street in Coeur d'Alene for the first time on Saturday, July 18, along with fellow White supremacists including the Ku Klux Klan (KKK). The Spokesman-Review joined the efforts to promote human rights by funding a major campaign titled "In It Together" with a series of newspaper articles and interviews discussing diversity and race relations. In addition, the newspaper also placed an insert of a large poster labeled "In It Together" encouraging everyone to place the poster in a window of their car or a window in their home. The KCTFHR organized a campaign that became known as the "Lemons to Lemonade" project. Donors gave funds to support human rights education for every minute of the march. Donations were made to multiple groups, including the Spokane chapter of the National Association for the Advancement of Colored People (NAACP). The Lemons to Lemonade project received national attention and contributions.

HEADLINE

"There are opportunities to acknowledge the day-by-day good deeds that go on in the name of human rights."—*Spokesman Review* Editorial. Kootenai County Task Force on Human Relations Scrapbooks 1992 by Molstead Library at North Idaho College

Instead of attending the Aryan Nations march in Coeur d'Alene on July 18, KCTFHR along with many civic and human rights organizations and individuals from Idaho and Washington held a counter rally. A large motorcade gathered at the Post Falls, Idaho Outlet Mall, in vehicles decorated with orange ribbons and signs for the drive to Gonzaga University in Spokane, Washington. Over 1,000 people attended the rally, celebrating human rights through speakers with messages affirming civil rights from individuals of diverse ethnic, racial, gender, age, and faith communities (T. Stewart, personal communication, August 19, 2019). The rally also included inspirational readings, music, materials, t-shirts, food, and free water provided by the Washington Water Power Company, now known as Avista. During the inter-faith service at St. Pius X Catholic Church in Coeur d'Alene on July 19, there was a joint Spokane/Coeur d'Alene Choir performance and community building messages.

In a 2009 response to the hate fliers that were being distributed throughout the region, the KCTFHR organized a press conference and rally at the Washington/Idaho border. There were 19 speakers at the August 21 KCTFHR press conference (Kootenai County Task Force on Human Relations,, History, n.d.). Speakers included representatives from the region's city police chiefs and mayors, the head of law enforcement for the Coeur d'Alene Tribe, the Spokane County Sheriff Ozzie Knezovich, the Kootenai County Prosecutor Barry McHugh. Master of Ceremonies and cofounder of the KCTFHR Tony Stewart, began the press conference with the warning: "We reject the hate and will aggressively prosecute all hate crimes" (T. Stewart, personal communication, August 19, 2019). As reported in the Coeur d'Alene Press (2009), others followed with statements including

> "We will not be known as places that allow hatred to dwell," stated Spokane Mayor Mary Verner.

> "We live in the best place in the world. Our quality of life depends on how we care for each other and how we protect our human rights," said Coeur d'Alene Mayor Sandi Bloem.

> Barry McHugh, the chief prosecutor for Kootenai County, Idaho declared: "When crimes are committed, it's our duty and obligation to prosecute to the full extent of the law."

> "We don't want anyone else to go through what the Native Americans went through for hundreds of years," stated Keith Hutchinson, Coeur d'Alene Tribe Police Chief.

KCTFHR organizers of the event, Christie Wood and Tony Stewart, in calling for the event stated: "Although we recognize and support the First Amendment right to free speech, we cherish the belief that where there's hate speech, good speech is essential and good speech will win in the end. We know that it comforts the people of the Inland Northwest and minorities in particular when we speak out as a unified people" (Coeur d'Alene Press, 2009). Following the press conference and rally, the leafleting of neighborhoods ceased for many months (T. Stewart, personal communication, August 19, 2019).

POINTS TO PONDER

Tony Stewart emphasizes speaking out against hate when it arises as a primary way to curtail hate within a community. How effective do you think community demonstrations against hate are at changing people's perspective and susceptibility on/to hate? Is the point to change perspectives?

The *Spokesman-Review* columnist Dave Oliveria shared an anecdote as to the effectiveness of the event from a mother of a family from Hattiesburg, Mississippi that was visiting the area on the day of the press conference. Oliveria said "The mother, Jackie Bland, upon her return to Hattiesburg, Mississippi wrote in a letter-to-the-editor of the Hattiesburg American newspaper these words: 'I thought this reaction by local leadership was astonishing as I was from the South and had never witnessed leadership calling out such acts. I also thought how wonderful it is for leaders to set the tone to what is and is not acceptable behavior'" (T. Stewart, personal communication, August 19, 2019).

HEADLINE

"Along with the leaders who turned out Rhursday came ordinary citizens ranging from those with white hair to at least one with spiked hair."— John Craig with The Handle. Article: Hundreds turn out to oppose hate groups. Kootenai County Task Force on Human Relations Scrapbooks 1992 by Molstead Library at North Idaho College

During the summer of 2010, members of the Westboro Baptist Church (WBC), an anti-LGBT group out of Topeka, Kansas, announced it would be picketing in Spokane and Coeur d'Alene, Idaho. In part, the group was protesting North Idaho College's Falltheater stage production of the "Laramie Project," a play about the murder of Matthew Shepard who was a gay student in Wyoming (Boggs, 2010). The WBC protested first at several locations in Spokane, Washington. Kevin Graman (2010), of the Spokesman-Review wrote "There's nothing like an extremist hate group to bring out the best in Spokane residents." Although 600 people counter protested near the location of the WBC pickets adjacent to the Gonzaga University campus, a counter protest was held on campus with a student sit-in, followed by speeches and rainbows of balloons. WBC moved on to picket at nearby Moody Bible College, Whitworth University, Eastern Washington University, a local high school and a Jewish synagogue. People at the synagogue, as with other locations, came together on common grounds to celebrate what they stood for, often with prayers, singing, dancing, and or speeches. "We're not here to confront them," said Elder Gary D'Angelo. "Confrontation doesn't do anything but cause more confrontation. In His words, He says 'overcome evil with good'" (Graman, 2010). The synagogue collected donations, one dollar for every minute of the Westboro protest, giving the funds to a nonprofit working to reduce drug and alcohol abuse and homelessness. The WBC would not return again until 2018.

THE WORK CONTINUES

After 19-months of the KCTFHR's work with a group of leaders in Spokane County, Washington, a press conference was held on March 8, 2016 that announced the formation of the Spokane County Human Rights Task Force. The new human rights group was created to be an action-driven force for civil and human rights in Spokane County, Washington. The new group was based on lessons learned from their sister organization, the KCTFHR.

Following a period of inaction and new challenges arising in the county, Leslie Waters and approximately 10 other Stevens County residents invited KCTFHR members Tony Stewart and Norm Gissel along with Southern Poverty Law Center blog writer Bill Morlin to a private meeting on November 18, 2016 to discuss plans for the renewal and reorganization of the Steven's County human rights organization. The Upper Columbia Human Rights Coalition drafted a set of new bylaws, elected officers and became active once again.

The political boundary between Spokane in eastern Washington and Coeur d'Alene in northern Idaho is not a barrier for partnerships and collaborations between the two communities standing up to hate. In July 2019, a Spokane, Washington based youth minister and his youth group attended a religious church service in Coeur d'Alene. They were targeted by an older man as they ordered ice cream at a Coeur d'Alene fast-food restaurant where the youth minister, who was of Hispanic ancestry, was physically attacked and shoved to the ground. The offender yelled racist words at the minister and the racially diverse youth. The KCTFHR became allies and advocates for the victims, working with the Coeur d'Alene Police and Kootenai County Prosecutor on behalf of the victims. On December 20, the defendant was found guilty of physical assault by a local jury and given the maximum sentence of six months in jail by the judge.

DISCUSSION QUESTIONS

1.

Briefly describe the situations in the case. What aspects of your description are judgments (value statements about what is good or bad) and what aspects are objective statements?

2.

What does the emphasis that White supremacist organizations put on recruiting youth to join their groups communicate about what their group thinks is important and what their concerns are? How does this information enable human rights groups to organize their counter-hate responses?

3.

Elizabeth Bullis is very unique in being the National Secretary for the Third Position. Why do you think the gender barrier is so defined in neo-Nazi groups?

4.

What role did the media play in countering hate in this case?

5.

What goal(s) can you envision for The Upper Columbia Human Rights Coalition. Brainstorm new strategies for reaching the goal(s). What are the strengths and limitations of each?

6.

What lessons do you take away from this case and how might you apply them in your own context?

REFERENCES

About Washington. (n.d.). Retrieved March 2, 2020, from historylink.org. https://historylink.org/File/20006

Associated Press. (1992, July 1). *Three Washington State Aryan Nations leaders quit.* Retrieved March 2, 2020, from The Lewiston Tribune. https://lmtribune.com/northwest/three-washington-state-aryan-nations-leaders-quit/article_a34972e0-b5ff-5c3d-8f7e-55264ab678c0.html

Cascade Range Mountains, United States. (2020). *Encyclopædia Britannica.* Retrieved from https://www.britannica.com/place/Cascade-Range]

Coeur d'Alene Press. (2009, August 22). *We will be here.* Retrieved from https://issuu.com/molsteadlibraryatnic/docs/kootenai_county_task_force_on_human_278d71f8ca1b23

Crawford, L, R., Garder, L, S., Mozzochi, J., & Taylor, L, R. (1994). Northwest imperative. *Internet Archive.* Retrieved from https://archive.org/stream/NorthwestImperative/Northwest_Imperative_djvu.txt

Former Aryan Nations Leader Arrested on Drug Charges in Arizona. (2017, May 22). Retrieved March 2, 2020, from Anti-Defamation League. https://www.adl.org/news/article/former-aryan-nations-leader-arrested-on-drug-charges-in-arizona

Graman, K. (2010, October 10). Spokane unites against Westboro's message of hate. *The Spokesman Review.* Retrieved from https://www.spokesman.com/stories/2010/oct/21/westboro-baptists-picket-draws-counterprotest/

KHQ-06. (2009, August 21). *"We will not be known as communities who tolerate hate" says Spokane mayor.* Retrieved https://www.khq.com/news/we-will-not-be-known-as-communities-who-tolerate-hate/article_82f4e441-63c1-595e-9afc-fc06a209708f.html

Label: Aryan Nations. (1992). Retrieved March 2, 2020, from Kitsapsun.com. https://web.kitsapsun.com/archive/1992/05-12/247727_label__aryan_nations.html

Map of US. (n.d.). *Maps of Washington State and its counties.* Retrieved March 2, 2020, from MapofUS.org. https://www.mapofus.org/washington/

Meagan, D. (2017, September 20). *Welcome to Hayden Lake, where white supremacists tried to build their homeland.* Retrieved from Medium. https://timeline.com/white-supremacist-rural-paradise-fb62b74b29e0

Morlin, B. (1996, February 17). Neo-Nazi moonlights as a ranger seasonal park service worker says he's no Longer with Aryans. *The Spokesman-Review*. Retrieved March 2, 2020, from www.spokesman.com. https://www.spokesman.com/stories/1996/feb/17/neo-nazi-moonlights-as-a-ranger-seasonal-park/

Office of Financial Management. (n.d.). *Population density by county*. Retrieved from https://www.ofm.wa.gov/washington-data-research/population-demographics/population-estimates/population-density/population-density-county#slideshow-11

Ostendorf, D. (2002). Christian Identity: An American heresy. *Journal of Hate Studies, 1*(1), 23–55. https://doi.org/10.33972/jhs.3

Richard, B. (1991, July 7). *Supremacists woo jobless loggers*. Retrieved March 2, 2020, from chicagotribune.com. https://www.chicagotribune.com/news/ct-xpm-1991-07-07-9103170458-story.html

Shulz, T. M. (2008, December 18). *Former deputy involved in drugs, minors & sex pleads for another chance*. Retrieved March 2, 2020, from Verde Independent. https://www.verdenews.com/news/2008/dec/18/former-deputy-involved-in-drugs-minors-sex-pleads/

Southern Law Poverty Center, Aryan Nations. (n.d.). Retrieved from Southern Law Poverty Center. https://www.splcenter.org/fighting-hate/extremist-files/group/aryan-nations

Up From Hatred. (1997, August 10). Retrieved March 2, 2020, from *Los Angeles Times*. https://www.latimes.com/archives/la-xpm-1997-aug-10-tm-21338-story.html

Washington. (n.d.). Retrieved March 2, 2020, from PM Capital. https://pmcapital.com/local/washington/

Washington Population 2019 (Demographics, Maps, Graphs). (2019). Retrieved from Worldpopulationreview.com. http://worldpopulationreview.com/states/washington-population/

Chapter 12

REFLECTIONS AND ACTIONS

The cases published here demonstrate how ordinary people can do extraordinary things to build just communities and stand against hate. These cases tell real stories from around the country, from Pennsylvania, to North Carolina, to Tennessee, to Wyoming, to Washington, of nonviolent strategies in which people took actions to determine how they would stand in solidarity with their neighbors and recognize the dignity and respect inherent in every person. Certainly, there are many examples across the country and around the world of people using nonviolent strategies to stand up to hate well beyond those discussed here. We have selected these particular cases because they have the common thread of leadership by the Kootenai County Task Force on Human Relations (KCTFHR). The leadership modeled by Diana Tanner ("Mother of the Task Force"), former Kootenai County Under-Sheriff Larry Broadbent, realtor Marshall Mend, former North Idaho College Political Science faculty member Tony Stewart, priest of St. Pius X Catholic Church Fr. Bill Wassmuth, and Attorney Norm Gissel inspire us today. It is these initial community members along with all those who joined in later years, who have maintained the group since 1981 without formal office space or staffing, that have stood the test of time, not only continuing their commitment to their own local region, but also supporting other communities across the country to develop their own nonviolent anti-hate strategies.

The community members who founded the KCTFHR in Coeur d'Alene, Idaho were motivated by attacks on people in their community, a swastika graffitied on a Jewish-run restaurant and later a local biracial family threatened by members of a White supremacist group. The work of the KCTFHR is ongoing, with members never letting their guard down as stewards in their own community. Early milestones for the group include their founding in 1981, the Gathering for Solidarity following the 1986 bombing of their president's home, and the 1998 Lemons to Lemonade counter initiatives. One of the most significant aspects in the history of the KCTFHR was the *Keenan v. Aryan Nations* civil trial in 2000, which resulted in a $6.3 million award against White supremacists and the creation of a peace park on the grounds of the former compound (Southern Poverty Law Center [SPLC], Keenan v Aryan Nations, n.d.). Although the KCTFHR has continued to be influential throughout the 21st century, the legacy of victory over hate can be celebrated once again with the sale of the peace park land to a private owner in 2020. The funds generated from the sale are committed to establishing the Gregory C. Carr Visiting Professor Chair endowment at North Idaho College as a means of sustaining human rights education. From White supremacy to peace park to funding in perpetuity for human rights education—the anti-hate legacy will live on.

Over the decades, the KCTFHR has successfully implemented a multitude of nonconfrontational approaches, focusing their energies on victim support, organizing counter events at alternative locations during hate group rallies and events, promoting state and federal human rights legislation, and coordinating educational programs and community events to advance human rights. According to one of the original founders Tony Stewart, "To carry out this work, we have determined never to remain silent. We can find no examples in history where silence has solved problems. Also, we will never engage in confrontation. We will follow the manner of Martin Luther King Jr. of doing something of our own elsewhere" (Hult, 2011, p. 1).

The work of countering hate is as relevant and necessary today as it was in the early days of the KCTFHR. A hate crime occurs when a crime (e.g., murder, arisen, vandalism) is motivated by bias and is formally defined as a "criminal offense against a person or property motivated in whole or in part by an offender's bias against a race, religion, disability, sexual orientation, ethnicity, gender, or gender identity" (Federal Bureau of Investigation [FBI], 2018). The FBI provides hate crime statistics documenting incidents and offenses, victims, offenders, types of locations, and jurisdictions. This information is made available through the Uniform Crime Reporting (UCR) program as reported by law enforcement agencies. According to the FBI, "hate crimes are the highest priority of the FBI's civil rights program because of the devasting impact they have on families and communities" (FBI, 2016).

Although the FBI, along with local law enforcement, play a vital role in countering hate, ordinary people can take action, too. Fundamentally, stopping hate crime before it starts is the best deterrent for transformation and lasting change. Many organizations provide resources that both educate people about these harms and support preventative strategies. Of note, the pyramid of hate developed by the Anti-Defamation League (ADL, 2018) as well as the 10 Stages of Genocide (Stanton, 2019) bring to our attention the importance of addressing the attitudes and language in our communities that are a cornerstone of how cultures do or do not value the dignity inherent in all people.

In the ADL's Pyramid of Hate, the underlying premise is that as one moves up from the bottom of the pyramid (bias attitudes to genocide) there is greater harm to people, and that higher levels in the pyramid (discrimination, hate crimes, and genocide) exist when the lower levels provide a basis for their existence. The age-old adage "sticks and stones may break my bones, but words will never hurt me" provides an interesting scaffolding for consideration. The adage assumes that insensitive remarks, noninclusive language, and misinformation are only words—without acknowledging that these words will in some cases provide bedrock for actions that grow out of these biases. Once communities allow negative stereotypes to normalize or flourish, it then makes bullying, epithets, and social avoidance more permissible. Attitudes (all X are terrorists), when combined with the perceived ability (I can use this language) and social norms (this is how we talk around here), lead to intention and action (discrimination, vandalism, threats, assault) as supported by in Ajzen's (1991) theory of planned behavior.

In our communities, what is good or valued is in large part determined by the culture. What stories are told and retold, who is identified as a hero or leader, what is celebrated, what is given resources (time, finances, space) define what is rewarded and aspired to in any community. The cases here tell leadership stories of everyday people who took action in ways that are structurally sustainable, responding both reactively and proactively to stop hate. By reading the real-life stories told here, you see how people formed local and regional human rights coalitions that were prepared to respond to hate with alternative activities during hate events (free movies, bowling, skating, go-cart, etc.) and counter-rallies at distant locations (music performances, singing, speeches, keynotes, prayers, proclamations, readings, food, activities) either at the same time as hate events or timed directly after a hate event to allow media to uncover the bias at the first event and immediately follow up with counter-narrative coverage.

What is a fundamental lesson here is that engaging with hate groups directly is counter to the nonviolent strategies proven in these case studies. Supporting free speech of all, while providing strength in numbers at counter-rallies with a broad range of leadership creates momentum toward community values and has time and again discouraged attitudes and norms that hatred in any manifestation is acceptable. It is an ongoing effort that requires vigilance, nurturing, and being proactive. Throughout the cases presented here, are also many examples of proactive means to celebrate justice and human rights. Following is a sampling of some of the nonviolent tactics directly from the cases:

- Announcements throughout the year, extending beyond single date coverage (KCTFHR Lemons to Lemonade campaign)
- Anti-hate/Human rights slogans
- Banquets (Annual)
- Birthday parties (Human Rights Task Force, the U.S. Constitution, Dr. Martin Luther King, Jr., etc.)
- Booths at local fairs
- Civil Rights Awards
- Civic Awards (e.g., Raoul Wallenberg Civic Award and All American City Award to Coeur d'Alene, ID)
- College Clubs (Human Equality)
- Communication campaigns (posters, billboards, brochures, ads, fliers, stickers etc.)
- Community sign on petitions
- Conferences
- Denounce acts of hate and hate ideologies publicly through social media
- Donations for human rights groups collected based on the duration of a hate gathering (parade, talk, etc.)
- Editorials

- Engaged leadership (politicians of all parties and levels, elected officials, education, business, chambers, nonprofit, education)
- Focus on Declaration of Independence and U.S. Constitution affirming human rights
- Hate incident reporting
- Interfaith services
- K-12 Programming (Annual)
- Legislation (Establish Human Right Commissions)
- Library collections on human rights (adult and children's sections)
- Media packages, praise for journalists' coverage
- Minority scholarships
- Motorcades between partners' locations (across county or state lines)
- Newspaper produced posters
- Newspaper series on human rights
- Resolutions and Proclamations (Invite similar efforts in other cities or states)
- Ribbon campaigns (displayed on clothing, cars, businesses, trees, etc.)
- Sit-Ins
- Statements of Commitment between Institutions of Higher Education and Community groups
- Symposiums
- Television programming
- Youth summer camps (Annual)

Understanding the deeper issues of human rights and hate is always of the utmost importance in civil society. In order to do this, we must all constantly work to refine our knowledge and experience with these issues. It is often difficult to engage with these topics, but there are many ways to get involved where dialogue may be moderated and cultivated. As you reflect on how you can take action to stand for human rights and take action against hate, consider the resource lists here as a starting point. The ensuing content provides samples of different tactics adapted from the educational and action-based resources that follow. Movements of hate are poignant, which is why anti-hate strategies must be well developed to effectively counter dehumanizing aggressions effectively. Although hate crimes and bias incidents are heartbreaking, these resources stand as evidence that there are positive steps that can be taken to address, resolve, and heal from hate filled experiences on an individual and communal level.

Start with caring for yourself

1. If you are the victim of a hate incident or crime, it is important to reach out beyond yourself to those who have the resources and knowledge to help you. (a) Reach out to law enforcement and file a police report even if you don't pursue a criminal investigation, it is imperative to document the incident. (b) Contact a civil rights organization for victim support and assistance. They may have a plethora of resources that can help you navigate throughout difficult times.
2. If you are White folk in the community, try to actively counter White fragility in order to not turn to defensive tactics when confronted and uncomfortable. Be malleable when called out, asking how racist narratives function.
3. Consider taking the 50 question Intercultural Development Inventory (IDI). This assesses intercultural competence and can provide tools to better engage with cultural difference.

Come together to listen with the purpose of learning

1. Host a civic dinner—food brings people together in an expression of community and culture. Celebrate being a part of the human family by throwing a party or gathering. It is important to connect with those in your community to establish strength and solidarity.
2. If you are capable and feel safe doing so, engage compassionately and listen to those who hold positions that marginalize others. This does not mean find your local Klansman, but rather associate with your family members, friends, coworkers, or casual acquaintances who may promote disrespectful ideologies.
3. If you are aware that a hate group is coming to your community, plan meetings to discuss the group's history, intentions, and value-sets so the community is less fearful and can be more resilient.

Organize

1. The key to a resilient community is having a strong, welcoming infrastructure that can provide strength if a crisis were to ever occur. To ensure this support system is there before hate happens is of the utmost importance to provide care for those effected. Institutions should be preemptive in countering hate. This includes setting high standards for inclusivity by setting the expectations early and keeping the messages consistent. It is important to curtail bad behavior, and it is equally as important to incentivize and reward good behavior.

2. Identify groups who would be energized to engage when hate rears its ugly head. Have just a few, two to three, core organizers who reach into their spheres of influence looking for people (10–20) who have some concern, connection, or involvement within the community. Try to establish a centralized and easily accessible meeting place. The meetings should follow the following order: introductions, the pitch, the planning, and closure. *Work smarter, not harder, and use wisdom and resources from other already established local and regional sources such as Human Rights and Civil Rights organizations.*

3. It is important to have a system put in place if a crisis were to ever occur. A recommended set of steps is put safety first, denounce the act, investigate, involve others when needed and applicable, work with the media, provide accurate information and dispel misinformation, support targeted individuals, seek justice, avoid blame, and promote healing.

SAMPLE LISTING OF EDUCATIONAL RESOURCES

1. ADL, n.d.. "Responding to Hate: Information and Resources." *Anti-Bias Education—Hate Crimes.* The ADL compiled this response advice for those targeted by a hate crime or incident. This section details two avenues in particular: (a) Reach out to law enforcement and file a police report regardless of whether there is a criminal investigation, so that there is record of the incident. (b) Contact a civil rights

organization for victim support and assistance. They have a plethora of resources and can assist in navigating this difficult time.

2. *Bard Center for the Study of Hate (BCSH)*. The BCSH brings together scholars from diverse to speak about the human capacity to hate and demonize others. It supports anti-hate internships and research for Bard students.

3. Big Think (2018, October 1). *Why "I'm Not Racist" Is Only Half the Story*, Robin DiAngelo. This is a video by a prominent anti-racist author and activist targeted toward White individuals for how to orient yourself with regard to your positionality as you strive to be antiracist. White folk in the community can actively combat their own White fragility in order to not turn to defensiveness tactics when confronted and uncomfortable. The work encourages malleability when called out for racism, asking how racist narratives function?

4. Brown, Rachel Hilary, et al. "Racial Equity Tools." *Strategies*. This website provides a reference list of resources to learn from and organizations to get involved in that are committed to hate crime prevention and response. It covers different variations of hate crimes and different targeted demographics.

5. Center for the Study of Hate and Extremism. Housed at California State University, San Bernardino, the Center for the Study of Hate and Extremism provides analysis and reports covering hate and extremism.

6. Center on Hate Bias and Extremism (CHBE). The CHBE advances awareness, understanding and prevention of hate, bias and extremism by providing research that will inform evidence-based policies and practices to promote a just and equitable society for all.

7. Community Relations Service (2001). "Hate Crimes: The Violence of Intolerance." Hate Crimes Bulletin, United States Department of Justice. This website provides information about the CRSs which is an arm of the Department of Justice. The services detailed are specifically equipped to design local solutions to combat hate crimes and other types of violence with information on hate crime statistics/definitions, case studies that show the work done by the CRS, details of the mechanisms used to combat hate, and contact information.

8. Global Project Against Hate and Extremism (GPAHE). GPAHE shines a light on racist and hateful activities, and through coordinated campaigns and an active transnational network, we expect to see a reduction in transnational extremist activities and an associated reduction in acceptance of bigoted ideologies.

9. Gonzaga Institute of Hate Studies (GIHS). The Gonzaga Institute for Hate Studies advances the academic field of Hate Studies and links the Gonzaga community with experts and key stakeholders worldwide through activities of inquiry, scholarship, and action-service; hosting a biennial International Conference on Hate Studies, publishing the *Journal of Hate Studies (JHS),* and acknowledging anti-hate activism and research through the Eva Lassman Awards.

10. International Network for Hate Studies (INHS). The INHS aims to provide an accessible forum through which anyone can engage with the study of hate and hate crime in a manner which is both scholarly and accessible to all. Academics, students, advocates and those working in the public and nongovernmental organization (NGO) sector

11. Journal of Hate Studies (JHS) is a peer-reviewed publication of the Gonzaga University Institute for Hate Studies. It is an open access international scholarly journal promoting the sharing of interdisciplinary ideas and research relating to the study of what hate is, where it comes from, and how to combat it. It presents cutting-edge essays, theory, and research that deepen the understanding of the development and expression of hate.

12. Kootenai County Task Force on Human Relations (KCTFHR). The KCTFHR provides education promoting positive human relations, supports people victimized by malicious harassment or hate crimes, promotes anti-hate legislation, monitors and documents hate incidents, celebrates human diversity, and opposes disiclination.

13. Not in Our Town (NIOT n.d.) "Community Response to Hate." In partnership with The Lawyers' Committee for Civil Rights Under Law, this is an action kit produced by NIOT. It details what one could use to assist in preventing and responding to hate crimes and bias incidents. Particularly, it goes over how to respond, what leaders in a community can do, provides film/media that can be used to educate and facilitate

discussion, and provides a resource guide that can be used to further address other questions that may arise.

14. Southern Poverty Law Center (SPLC, 2017, August 14) "Ten Ways to Fight Hate: A Community Response Guide." This community response guide is compiled by the SPLC that focuses on addressing the following claim and question: "Hate in America has become commonplace. What can we do to stop the hate?" It details 10 nuanced steps/ actions one can take to ensure they combat and don't contribute to the problem: Act, Join Forces, Support the Victims, Speak Up, Educate Yourself, Create an Alternative, Pressure Leaders, Stay Engaged, Teach Acceptance, and Dig Deeper.

15. Toole, Ken (1995, November). "What to Do When the Militia Comes to Town." Montana Human Rights Network, The American Jewish Community. This report provides comprehensive information on what to do combat the violence and intimidation that may ensue following a militia coming into your community. It details facts about the activity of militias across the country, actions that can be taken to inhibit the power of a militia group, and emphasizes the importance of research to being an effective combatant of militia violence. The main strategy is forming a community group—to learn more follow the link above.

16. Western States Center. "Confronting What Nationalism in Schools" This toolkit contains strategies to counter White nationalist organizing through sample scenarios that schools frequently encounter. Whether a student has been found passing out White nationalist flyers or buttons on school property, or more actively advocating for a "White pride" student group, the toolkit offers advice for parents, students, teachers, school administrators, and the wider community.

17. Willoughby, Brian. "Responding to Hate and Bias at School." A Guide for Administrators, Counselors, and Teachers, Teaching Tolerance. This report details how schools—with implications to wider institutions—should deal with hate and bias. As an institution, it is important to have a system put in place if a crisis were to ever occur. The process recommended is to put safety first, denounce the act, investigate, involve others when needed and applicable, work with the media, provide accurate information—and dispel misinformation, support targeted individuals, seek justice, avoid

blame, and promote healing. Moreover, the appendix provides different forms that can be used as the basis for implementing and organizing a response system.

SAMPLE LISTING OF ORGANIZATIONS AND INTERACTIVE RESOURCES

1. Civic Dinners. Food brings people together in an expression of community and culture and Civic Dinners is the platform that brings people together to have conversations that matter. To attend host a Civic Dinner, follow the link above; the loveablecity.org is a great resource that can help you host or join a dinner going on in your area.
2. Clamoring for Change. Clamoring for Change is a forum that promotes conversation over controversial topics and subjects to reduce polarization. Ultimately, it is a platform that encourages changing oneself—to be more tolerant and communicative—in order to change society.
3. Intercultural Competence Using the Intercultural Development Inventory (IDI). In order to assess the overall intercultural competence within an organization, businesses and institutions with workforces who engage with diverse demographics should have their employees/ volunteers/people take a 50 question questionnaire called the IDI. This questionnaire can help identify weaknesses or concerns exist within your workforce so that management effectively target those areas with tolerance training.
4. One Peoples Project. Organized by prominent anti-racist activist and organizer, Daryle Lamont, the One Peoples Project works to organize grassroot anti-facist resistance. To participate, you can join their Community Watch program to receive notice of hate activities in your area as well as information about the counter-organizing that would ensue.
5. Welcoming America. The key to a resilient community is having a strong, welcome infrastructure that can provide strength if a crisis were to ever occur. To ensure this support system is there before hate happens is of the utmost importance to provide care for those effected. The Welcoming America Model is an incredibly valuable footprint for what this looks like—particularly in relation to immigrants and refugees.

REFERENCES

Ajzen, I. (1991). The theory of planned behavior. *Organizational Behavior and Human Decision Processes, 50*(2), 179–211. https://doi.org/10.1016/0749-5978(91)90020-t

Anti-Defamation League. (2018). *Pyramid of Hate*. Retrieved from https://www.adl.org/sites/default/files/documents/pyramid-of-hate.pdf

Anti-Defamation League. (n.d.). *Responding to hate: Information and resources*. Retrieved April 19, 2020, from https://www.adl.org/education/resources/tools-and-strategies/responding-to-hate-information-and-resources

Big Think. (2018, October 1). *Why "I'm not racist" is only half the story | Robin DiAngelo* [Video]. YouTube. Retrieved from https://www.youtube.com/watch?v=kzLT54QjclA

centerCivic Dinners. (n.d.). Retrieved April 19, 2020, from Civic Dinners. https://about.civicdinners.com/

Community Relation Service, United States of Department of Justice. (2001, December). Hate crime: The violence of intolerance. *Hate Crime Bulletin*. Retrieved from www.justice.gov. https://www.justice.gov/archive/crs/pubs/crs_pub_hate_crime_bulletin_1201.htm

Federal Bureau of Investigation. (2016). *Civil rights*. Retrieved from Federal Bureau of Investigation. https://www.fbi.gov/investigate/civil-rights

Federal Bureau of Investigation. (2018). *Hate crimes*. Retrieved from Federal Bureau of Investigation. https://www.fbi.gov/investigate/civil-rights/hate-crimes

Hult, K. (2011, September). *Fig Tree—Kootenai County task force 30 years*. Retrieved from www.thefigtree.org. http://www.thefigtree.org/sept11/090711KootenaiTFHR.html

Not in Our Town. (n.d.). *Community response to Hate*. Retrieved April 19, 2020, from www.niot.org. https://www.niot.org/stop-hate-action-kits/community-response-to-hate

Southern Poverty Law Center, Keenan v. Aryan Nations. (n.d.). Retrieved from Southern Poverty Law Center. https://www.splcenter.org/seeking-justice/case-docket/keenan-v-aryan-nations

Southern Poverty Law Center, Ten Ways to Fight Hate: A Community Response Guide. (2017). Retrieved from https://www.splcenter.org/20170814/ten-ways-fight-hate-community-response-guide

Stanton, H. G. (2019). *Ten stages of genocide*. Retrieved from Genocidewatch.net. http://genocidewatch.net/genocide-2/8-stages-of-genocide/

Teaching Tolerance, A Project of The Southern Poverty Law Center. (2017). Responding to Hate and bias at school a publication of teaching tolerance. *Teaching Tolerance Org*, 1–52. Retrieved from https://www.tolerance.org/sites/default/files/2017-07/Responding%20to%20Hate%20at%20School%202017.pdf

Toole, K. (1995). What we do when the militia comes to town. *The American Jewish Committee*, 1–38. Retrieved from https://mhrn.org/publications/whattodo_militia.pdf

CPSIA information can be obtained
at www.ICGtesting.com
Printed in the USA
LVHW060823271021
701605LV00001B/1

9 781792 460470